Looking at Cities

Allan B. Jacobs

Harvard University Press
Cambridge, Massachusetts, and London, England
1985

Copyright © 1985 by the President and Fellows of Harvard College
All rights reserved
Printed in the United States of America
10 9 8 7 6 5 4 3 2 1

This book is printed on acid-free paper, and its binding materials
have been chosen for strength and durability.

Designed by Marianne Perlak

Library of Congress Cataloging in Publication Data

Jacobs, Allan B.
  Looking at cities.

  Bibliography: p.
  Includes index.
  1. City planning—Methodology. I. Title.
HT166.J262 1985   307'.12   84-19247
ISBN 0-674-53891-9

To the memory of my mother, Bess
and to Hy and Freda
and Amy, Matthew, and Janet

Acknowledgments

Students generated this book. In the spring of 1975 a group of students, led by Liza Smith, asked me to show them San Francisco. That seemed a strange request. Didn't students of city and regional planning normally spend time walking in, looking at, wondering about, and enjoying cities? And wasn't San Francisco, just across the bay, as good a city in which to do that as one could find in North America? Although I did not think of myself as a tour guide, I took them, and we enjoyed the long afternoon. Most of the locations we visited were associated with major issues or large projects or were in the process of changing. We talked about areas that were vulnerable to change and about what might be ahead, based upon what we could see, in some parts of the city.

Three of the students asked me to give an experimental course the next year on how to look at a city. I was reluctant because it did not seem a proper academic activity, but I did lead such a course. That was the beginning of student involvement in this work. Over the years students wrote papers on specific environmental clues, made case studies of specific neighborhoods, and studied the field observation methods of other professions. They questioned and challenged my work, as I did theirs.

More than a hundred students took part in that work, more than I can name here, but I do want to acknowledge their assistance. Five of them have been particularly helpful. Charlie Bryant helped me organize the work in its early stages. He and Julia Gould did an excellent study of learning about ethnic boundaries through observation. Julia searched the libraries for relevant literature, and, with Janet Linse, set up field

studies. Janet, Leslie Gould, and Terry O'Hare under-
took case studies with me and helped report them.
Terry prepared the maps of the cities that appear in the
book. Cara Seiderman helped proofread and prepare
the index.

Leslie Gould worked on this book from start to
finish—on outlines, work programs, case studies, and
research. She reviewed and helped edit each draft. Her
creative contributions to this book are beyond counting. For five years she has been an inspiring confidante
and a very close friend.

The case studies—those reported on here and others
— proved to be more important than I had anticipated.
They required time, patience, and help from local
professionals. Patricia Columbe reviewed the study of
Naglee Park, San Jose. Ralph Bolton, Martin Griesel,
April Laskey, Dan Lenz, and Charles Lohre reviewed
and commented on the Cincinnati case. In Italy Giuseppe Campos Venuti of Bologna, Maurizio Marcelloni
and Lorenzo Bruno of Rome, and Guido Martinotti and
Adolfo Carvelli of Milan put up with me, helped me,
and taught me. The Italian chapter could not have
been written without them. Other reviewers in other
cities were James McKellar in Calgary, Alberta; Yale
Rabin and Warren Boeschenstein in Charlottesville,
Virginia; Sally Williams and Howard Jennings in Rich-
mond, Virginia; Martin Boat and Ernie Vivakis in East
Palo Alto; Christopher Buckley in Oakland; Dianne A.
Jackson in Sacramento; George Osner and William
Nichols in Modesto; and Charna Staten in San Francisco. My colleagues and I interviewed many people
who were enlightening, none more so than Dr. Harvey
Salans, who advised me almost poetically about medi-
cal diagnosis.

Financial aid and time to work on this book came
from a number of sources. The University of California
awarded me research funds and the time I needed in
the form of a sabbatical leave. A Guggenheim fellow-
ship provided funds and additional time to research,
write, and undertake case studies in Italy. The American Academy in Rome was a magnificent place to
work, thanks to Sophie Consagra, as was Dolf

Schnebli's home in Agno, Switzerland. Bill and Mary Jane Brinton helped me financially, without conditions, as they have in the past. The Institute of Urban and Regional Development graciously provided help in preparing the manuscript.

Bob Cajina and the staff of the Department of City and Regional Planning at Berkeley have always been supportive of my work by permitting me to do whatever I want. Mary Gizdich and Constance McCurry worked on early drafts of chapters, and Nene Ojeda of the Institute of Urban and Regional Development typed the manuscript at least three times with good humor and with dispatch, no small achievement.

Many professional and academic colleagues have read and commented on all or parts of the work. Jack Kent, always a positive, probing critic, read and commented on the early drafts. Manuel Castells and Peter Hall advised me throughout. Mark Baldassare, Barry Checkoway, John Kriken, Tom Aidala, and Mike Teitz reviewed parts of the work. Donald Appleyard and I had two or three discussions about the book before his death. Individually and collectively, their reviews improved the book.

Amy Jacobs was a very special consultant. She questioned me over and over about the logic of what I was trying to say and insisted that the language be understandable. She forced me to think more clearly about the substance of observation and what can be learned by looking. I thank her profusely.

Contents

Looking at Cities

1 Starting to Look

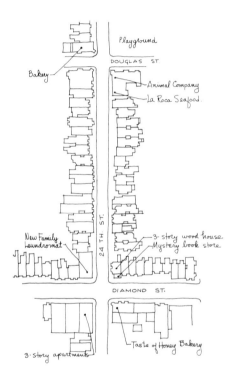

You can tell a lot about a city by looking. When I was visiting a new housing development in Tangshan, China, in late 1981, I noticed that many of the ground floor units had makeshift grates or grilles around the windows and porches. I commented to my Chinese colleague that in America those grilles would indicate a safety problem. He said that in China they meant the same thing.

Consider, briefly, what we can see by walking along a few streets in a San Francisco neighborhood, and what we can learn. A three-story, square, wood-framed house, painted a not very fresh yellow ocher, stands at the northwest corner of Diamond Street and 24th Street.[1] Though the house is clearly not one of San Francisco's Victorians, there is a Victorian feeling to some of the details. Maybe it was built at the turn of the century or as late as 1920. Stairs climb to a small second-level entry porch with two doors into the house. The two house numbers, 748 and 750, indicate that there are probably two dwelling units. The main part of the house is set back a bit from the sidewalk, but a small addition to the original building brings it to the sidewalk line. The lettering on the window says "San Francisco Mystery Book Store." Above the store windows the yellow ocher paint silhouettes the distinctive shapes of earlier signs that have been removed. The shapes remind one of once-familiar signs: Meadow Gold dairy products? Perhaps this was once a corner mom-and-pop grocery store.

The windows on the top floor of the house are double-hung in a wood-frame sash, the upper half divided into three panes. They are probably the original windows. Those on the second floor are newer alumi-

num casements. Pockmarks in the aluminum suggest that the windows have been there for a long time.

Something about the yellow ocher paint attracts attention. A closer look at a corner, where the paint is cracked and peeling, shows that this is very thick paint with a grit in it, a kind we've heard advertised by large paint companies. The ads promise that this new paint is twenty times thicker than ordinary paint and will last a long, long time, eliminating the need for costly regular painting. They promise that it will seal leaks, that it is self-cleaning, that it will not crack, that it is guaranteed, and that favorable credit terms are available. In the past, similar claims have been made for asbestos shingles, permastone, and aluminum siding. But there *are* cracks in this paint, and it *is* peeling. Why do people buy these materials? They may think that the new paint or siding is better than the old or more pleasing. Or the prospect or not having to shell out all that money for a new coat of paint every five or so years appeals. The large companies that sell such materials often offer plans for small monthly payments over a number of years, which may be appealing if cash is in short supply. But now there are cracks. Where are the people who made the guarantee? What happens to the water that gets into the cracks?

As we walk farther on Diamond Street, the next four houses are similar to each other and of no familiar architectural style. Next are two small Victorians, then two in a style like that of the four, then a larger Italianate Victorian at the corner. This array suggests that development occurred over some time, perhaps from before the turn of the century into the teens, and was carried out by several small builders.

Changes in the original structures are apparent when we compare one with another. Putting asbestos siding on one of the group of four required the removal of some trim details. Two have had garages added, two have been painted recently. The roofing on all of them looks good; the shingles lie flat. All of the first four houses are single-family, as attested by single light meters and house numbers that are visible from the street.

All the house fronts on the block pace off to 25 feet wide, and the sides, determined by pacing at the corner, come to about 33 feet. That is not very large: 825 square feet for two floors. Housing for working-class, blue-collar, middle- or lower-middle-income families?

Back at the intersection of 24th and Diamond is the New Family Laundromat on the southwest corner. An old sign indicates that a "Washateria" was there earlier, and a still older sign tells of the Diamond Bakery. Through a second-floor window of this simple, two-story, stucco building, we see a white-haired man who looks to be in his sixties. He rises and turns off a television set. Next to the laundromat on Diamond are two two-story buildings that once had stores in them. Now, white curtains and blinds behind the large shop windows suggest people in residence. Len's Super Market, on the first floor of the next house, looks like a classic mom- and-pop grocery.

Most of the men and women at the intersection seem to be in their late fifties or sixties. Many have gray or white hair. Some wait at a bus stop, holding small packages. They are dressed functionally rather than stylishly: straight wool coats with simple collars, double-knit slacks in dark colors. One or two wear hats. One lady wears a rust-colored coat and fairly bright red pants.

At the third corner four or five girls go in and out of the Taste of Honey — Natural Bakery (good smells, arty lettering on the sign). Are the girls away from school, at lunch? Next to the bakery, on Diamond, a new store, Auntie Pasta, announces that it will open soon. When the buses go by, the intersection is very noisy. A young boy pedals a low-rider plastic tricycle. All of the people are white except for an Asian (not Chinese) girl. At the corners the curbs are concrete, fairly new and un-stained, with ramps for handicapped people. Away from the corners the curbs are granite.

On the fourth corner is a three-story multifamily residential building. It is mostly stucco, with no architectural details except some shingles for decoration. The windows are dark aluminum casements, with similar white drapes in all. A small entrance and large garage doors face the street. A building of the 1970s.

As we walk west on 24th for one block, we see many houses—as many as eighteen on one side of the street—on 25-foot lots. There is only one group of three similar houses in a row. Most are two-story, with some one- and three-stories. Architectural styles vary greatly, and the age range could be from the turn of the century to the 1950s; siding materials are wood, stucco, and some brick. Most buildings have one or two units. One house with two entry doors has four recently added mailboxes. The diversity continues: some windows are clean, others dirty; neat white curtains in one house, a makeshift window covering, perhaps a tablecloth in the next; safety devices on some doors and windows, but with no regularity. One house has relatively new siding shingles. The joinery is a bit ragged, especially at the window frames. It looks as though it may have been done by the owner to improve the house. On other houses the Victorian detailing has been removed and replaced with stucco. Two or three houses have been painted recently. One is for sale. A look between some houses shows large rear yards.

At one house two young men are carrying sheet-metal construction materials from a truck into the garage, where much more material is stored. The lettering on the truck says Shasta Mechanical Construction. At the next corner, Douglas, there are commercial uses. The La Roca Seafood Restaurant, which offers a meal for ten dollars, has cloth tablecloths, and the napkins are set in wine glasses. The Animal Company and the Noble Pies Cafe and Bakery are on diagonally opposite corners of the intersection. The bakery building was recently painted, including the thin roof shingles. The workmanship and paint grade are good but not the best.

We end this walking trip at the Noe Valley Play Area, across Douglas from the Animal Company. The play equipment, planting, tiles, and concrete work are relatively new, but there is an old storage and toilet building and one old tree. The net on the tennis court is metal screening, and the fence does not completely surround the court. Some children and a teacher are talking in one corner of the park.

We saw a lot in that thirty-five-minute walk, more than I can record in a few pages. And we learned some things about the area that we had not known. We conclude that the first houses in the neighborhood were built somewhat before the turn of the century and that development continued, a few houses at a time, by many small-scale builders, over a long period. The houses are not large, suggesting that working-class families lived in them. The owners of the one- and two-unit and the few multifamily buildings probably lived there with their families and maintained them. Blue-collar workers might have worked in the industrial areas to the east, at the end of 24th Street, or south of the downtown area. Public transit to those areas would have been easy. Office workers would have worked downtown. The older people we saw may not be the original owners and tenants, but they have been there for a long time. All of this suggests a quiet neighborhood where people have tried to "keep up," modestly maintaining and improving their properties. The houses show no evidence of major physical problems.

There are signs of change, past and present. There are indications that some residents are young people with modest incomes, like the flower children of the late 1960s or the environmental activists of recent years. Younger people, some with children, continue to move in, and some are upgrading the properties. There are new, trendy stores. Young, professional, downtown-oriented people may be replacing the older people, and "gentrification" may be an issue. In a city with an office-oriented economy we can expect more young business professionals to seek this area, as well as people from the large homosexual community nearby.

The old people will die or leave, but slowly. It seems a socially and economically mixed area, but so far, change does not seem to have been fast.

Not all clues are as easily read as the window grilles in China or the houses along 24th Street, nor are their meanings so easily understood. But conscious, careful, purposeful looking, accompanied by continuous questioning of the meanings of what one sees, can tell a lot about a city or neighborhood. Observation can tell something about the history and present dynamics of an area: when and for whom it was built; what physical, social, and economic changes have taken place; who lives there now; what major issues and problems exist; whether the area is vulnerable to rapid change and, if so, what kind. One can see how the area is related to the larger urban setting; and one can even predict what changes may be expected. Observing may not reveal everything about an area, but it can tell a great deal.

Most people do not look at a city or a neighborhood or even a city block the way we have just looked at 24th Street between Diamond and Douglas, but they do look. People who live in cities, including urban planners, developers, bankers, social activists, city watchers, and politicians, take cues from their physical environments every day, knowingly or not, and they often base their actions on those messages. They should therefore learn to look carefully. The purpose of this book is to show how professional planners and others in urban environments can use field observation as an important diagnostic tool. One of my purposes is to help everyone look more keenly, more caringly at the cities where we live.

Visual diagnosis is an important tool in many professional disciplines. A first step in a medical examination is the doctor's initial observation of the patient based on observable symptoms as well as the history. My doctor explained that the first part of a physical examination was to "look, feel, and then pat." He was surprised to hear that observation was not a well-established and systematic part of urban planning.

Archeologists at a potential dig site look for clues before starting to excavate, and much of their analysis of what they find is based on looking. Geologists look at a hill form or cut section and judge the earth-forming processes that shaped it. Structural engineers look for cracks and settling in buildings and bridges to help predict how and when the structures may fail. Foresters can tell about past and future weather cycles by looking at trees.[2] People concerned with the natural environment and with landscape architecture contend that "the man-made landscape provides strong evidence of the kind of people we are, and were, and are in the process of becoming."[3] Grady Clay, in *Closeup: How to Read the American City*, relies heavily on his visual experiences and accumulated knowledge to interpret cities.[4]

Site observation plays a large role in developers' decisions to move ahead, or not, on major projects. Any number of observable indicators are used in such a decision, including accessibility, surrounding land uses, nearby successful development, parks, level of street activity, types of people, climate, and similarity to known examples. If the project is financially feasible, the developer's assessment of the site may be mainly visual — he likes it or he doesn't — and subsequent research is done to support that instinct.

But observation as a primary method of inquiry and analysis has lost favor with urban planning professionals in recent years. It is thought to be too subjective as a basis for serious action compared to more quantifiable, statistically oriented methods.[5] We may say there is "no substitute for a first-hand look," but it is not always clear that we believe it, especially when so much information is available from secondary sources like the census and it is so easy to manipulate. Professionals and academics are often uncomfortable with findings based on observation rather than on "hard data," and yet so much of what they speak of concerns what they have seen.

City planners and designers who are interested in the myriad creative possibilities inherent in an urban community need first-hand experiences. Observation helps recall other places, thus triggering ideas about possible ways to bring about desirable change.

I would like to bring to urban planning a greater understanding of how to look at and interpret urban phenomena and to develop a research method that planners can use. Seeing people and their environments is quite different from learning about them second hand. Ideas of the poorness or wealth of a population suggested by income statistics may not be borne out by observations of those people in their daily lives. There is a great difference between reading age statistics and seeing people with gray or white hair, carrying small packages, waiting for buses, using the laundromat, as we saw at 24th and Diamond streets. *Seeing* twelve boarded-up houses one after another in North Sacramento has a much more powerful impression than being *told* that there are quite a few vacant houses in an older area. Planners tend to be more careful in deciding on policies and actions when they associate real people's faces and images of real places with the decisions.

Presumably, urban planners are concerned with documenting change in order to anticipate and act on the consequences, with guiding change, encouraging it, or stopping it. Field observation permits identifying the changes that are taking place earlier than is usually possible through other research methods. The data that are so often the basis for analyzing urban issues, and even "recent" surveys of physical and socioeconomic conditions, do not usually tell of the more dynamic changes happening in neighborhoods and city districts. An early awareness that an area is vulnerable to rapid physical deterioration in difficult economic times or to property speculation that will bring pressures for changes in land uses or for dislocation of people can be useful. Those who are in positions to respond to that change or encourage it can at least be ready.

No public agency or private firm has the funds or time to undertake all the research they want to do. Field observation can spot problems or apparent abnormalities on which to focus more intensive research efforts. In the late 1970s two students, walking through a low- to moderate-income area of San Francisco where change had not been a concern, spotted some clues that made them wonder whether concentrated improvement and speculation had already started. The students could see extensive interior remodeling being done on many buildings, much of it done by young men, perhaps gays, on weekends. (Gay men are a significant source of property upgrading efforts in the city.) Two or three commercial establishments—a coffee house and an interior design store (by appointment only)—seemed out of place in an area of low-income minorities and many elderly people. On other properties the new work seemed superficial—cheap paint, inexpensive cabinets to modernize kitchens and bathrooms, work that "showed" rather than repair of more significant foundation and roof problems. These properties displayed signs for two real estate firms known for high-turnover speculation. The observations prompted the students to do more detailed research on house sales, building permits, price changes, population shifts, and the like, all of which confirmed the observations. Observation, then, can direct research and action. A major premise of this book is that the more conscious we are of the relationships between what is observed and what actions are taken, the more likely we are to have better, more humane, more livable cities.

Often, however, messages taken from the physical environment have been read wrong, and programs based on them have been misguided. So it is important to proceed with caution and to develop attitudes of looking that minimize error. Often when we look at cities, what we see makes us uncomfortable: houses badly in need of paint, dirty windows with makeshift curtains or none at all, broken siding or trim, dark entryways, rubbish, overgrown yards, dirty streets, abandoned cars. The people, may make us feel uneasy: they may look different from the people we are accustomed to—poorly dressed, children running wild, derelicts. It is a short step from observing something that makes us uncomfortable to associating what is seen with all kinds of social pathologies—associations

that may well be incorrect. A next step may be an attempt to cure or eliminate the problem or illness.

What I am contending is that planners have often taken drastic actions in city neighborhoods because something about them was offensive, that it has often been the visual perception of the environment rather than some documented pathology, that has triggered the actions. Without being aware of it, we translate visual observations that cause us discomfort into social and economic problems, then we proceed to solve those problems by destroying the offending environment. The "we" have generally been the "haves" or the majority culture and their professional representatives.

It is not hard to find examples to make this point. In San Francisco's redevelopment heyday in the 1960s, the census designated as seriously substandard fewer than one-fourth of the units in five of the seven earliest redevelopment projects.[6] Detailed studies of housing conditions in the city's so-called Western Addition area indicated that it was more economic to rehabilitate than to tear down the buildings. But local authorities insisted on labeling such areas as slums and on removing their buildings and people. Boston's West End may be another example of the clearing of an environment that was basically sound, though visually offensive to some. Certainly many city areas that have been drastically changed were indeed physically dilapidated and had economic problems that made clearance necessary. But my contention is that in both types of cases it was the observed environment that made the area a target for action, that too often the visual message was misinterpreted, and consequently the action was misguided.

I believe that it will be easy to make those mistakes again. As part of a normal classroom exercise I ask graduate students to undertake studies of building condition, nothing more. Since about 1980 students repeatedly have translated observations such as missing materials, old and flaking paint, sagging porches, taped over window cracks, and unkempt yards into action-oriented categories such as "possible clearance" and "needs major repair." In the 1970s, socially aware students who made such observations did not come to those conclusions. On field excursions I find that students, nonprofessionals, and professionals all translate psychologically uncomfortable surroundings into building conditions that require demolition or some other drastic action. The next generation of professionals is likely to make the same kinds of decisions about the urban environment, based on observation, that the redevelopment-minded generation of the 1940s and 1950s made. Informed, careful, questioning observation can help avoid that.

Different people see and interpret what they see in different ways, depending on a host of variables. Some of these are situational—buildings tend to look less good on a cloudy day than on a sunny day—and others have to do with the observer's focus—development or on preservation, for example. Probably the most important variables are the values observers bring with them and everything that makes up their personal experience. People do not observe with a blank mind; they come with certain expectations, based on their values and past experiences.[7] Also there may be differences in people's judgment about actual physical attributes of an environment, for example, residents' perceptions of air quality may not agree with objective measurements of it.[8] People construct mental maps that enable them to acquire, organize, recall, and manipulate information about their physical environments. The maps vary from group to group and individual to individual.[9]

Not only do environments frequently operate below our level of awareness, they also provide more information than we can process.[10] So we inevitably miss some clues. And much as we might like to, we cannot stand apart from the environment; we must participate in it.[11] So regardless of the purposes of observation, or its scale, mode, or process, the experiences and values we bring to the task color what we see. We cannot observe with objectivity.

We should we do, then? One response is to give up, to forget the whole business, since no one interpretation of the environment can be right. But I do not believe we can do that even if we want to. Consciously understanding that each observer looks at a neighborhood differently from everyone else may be the best start to a solution. That understanding suggests taking messages from the environment cautiously. It points up the necessity of using this method along with other methods — something that is normally done in any case — and points to the desirability of doing field observation with other people.

The issue of how values and experience influence observation will continue to arise. Of course I bring my own values and biases to observing and interpreting what I see. I believe that cities ought to be magnificent, beautiful places to live, places where people can be fulfilled, places of freedom, love, ideas, excitement, quiet, and joy. Cities should be the ultimate manifestation of a society's collective achievements. City planning is the art of helping cities to become and to stay that way.

My philosophy of city planning stems from a belief that the people of a city have a right to say what they want their community to be — physically, socially, economically, culturally — and the responsibility to go out and achieve those goals.

City planning involves managing the process of change, so it makes sense, I think, to be constantly on the lookout for signs of change. In my looking I seek to identify who might benefit by changes and who might be hurt. I tend to mistrust big, centrally determined changes, preferring those in which many, many people can take part. Observation is an easily accessible way for almost anyone to become informed about change and then to take part in managing it.

It is more than a personal value or preference that leads me to the conclusion that walking is by far the best way to look at cities. There are other acceptable modes of observation, which can be appropriate, depending on the size and type of area, and the purpose of looking. But nothing replaces looking while on foot. The speed of other modes makes it difficult to see and explore details.

The walking observer can control the pace and the amount of time of looking at any particular scene more directly and more easily than when driving or riding. Walkers have nothing else to do in terms of locomotion so they can concentrate on looking. Mobility is maximized: a person can walk around a park or on public stairs, even look into someone's backyard.

Walking allows the observer to be in the environment with no barriers between the eyes and what is seen. The sensual experience—noises, smells, even the feel of things—is a real part of walking. There is more than you can take in: sights, sounds, smells, wondering what it might be like to live there, what it used to be like, and much more. It is an exciting, heady business.

2 Observing and Interpreting Naglee Park

We have come to an area of San Jose, California, called Naglee Park.[1] Our purpose is to determine the extent to which we can piece together what we see to find out about the history and dynamics of the area. When was it built? For whom? What physical, social, and economic changes have taken place? Who lives there now? What are the major issues and problems? Is the area vulnerable to rapid change? How might it change in the future?

Normally, as city planners, real estate developers, investors, traffic engineers, or concerned citizens, we would not try to answer these questions by observation alone. Someone would have told us something about the area beforehand, or we would be checking out a problem that had arisen, or we would have known Naglee Park from daily experience and would match what we see with statistical data about the area. This, however, is a test case. What can two strangers to San Jose learn about Naglee Park in three hours? At the start we know only that San Jose is the center of a rapidly growing urban area, that much of its development replaced orchards in what is considered "urban sprawl," and that the electronics industry is booming in this part of the Bay area, some fifty miles south of San Francisco.

We drive south from Berkeley, arriving in Naglee Park at about 10 A.M. on a warm Friday in late June 1981. First we drive around the area briefly, observing that on Santa Clara Street we are not too far from downtown San Jose to the west, as indicated by a concentration of tall buildings, and that San Jose State University borders the area on 10th Street. We drive east through the neighborhood, looking up and down

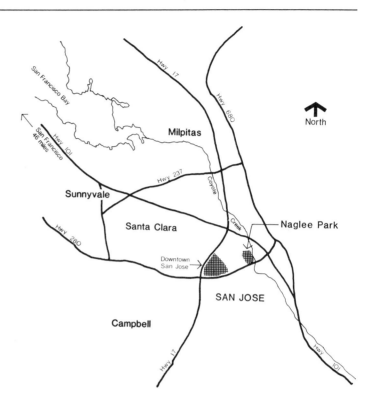

NAGLEE PARK – SAN JOSE

the numbered cross streets as we pass. Multifamily units along 11th Street soon give way to older homes, apparently single-family. We look for a focal point, such as a local shopping street, as a good place to start walking, but we don't see one. We continue to 17th Street at the eastern edge of the area and park the car in the shade.

At 17th and San Antonio, which is a residential street, a sign states that a parking permit is required between September and June from 9 A.M. to 1 P.M. Those are school months and busy class hours, so we conclude that the influence of the university probably extends this far and that student parking has been a bother to residents. Do the parking regulations testify to organized resident concerns, expressed successfully at City Hall?

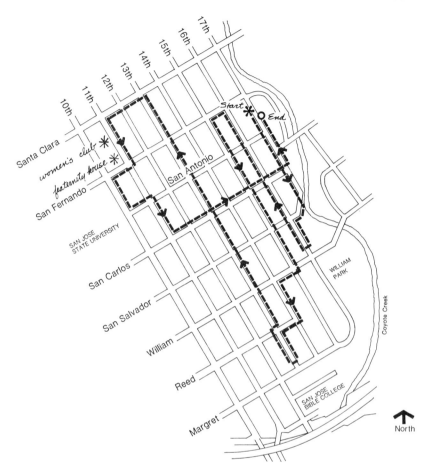

WALKING ROUTE IN NAGLEE PARK – SAN JOSE

Scale

The housing on 17th Street is from different periods: most of it earlier than the 1930s plus a few post–World War II houses. These look newer and are more modest in scale, with less detail. The houses on the east side of the street are larger and in better repair than those on the west side, perhaps because they abut a ravine and creek to the rear, considered a choice location. On that side of the street we see two older women sitting on the side patio of a well-maintained home. The street trees are large, and the houses are well set back from the sidewalk. We have a feeling that the people on the west side have moved in more recently and perhaps are younger. We see a moving van and

furnishings being carried into a vacant house. The belongings do not seem very substantial. Some pieces look a bit frayed at the edges, older and more used than what more well-to-do people would have, and they do not all match in style. Are these people connected to the university?

The houses on 16th Street north of East William Street appear to be single-family homes. The level of maintenance is not the best, and the yards are not as well cared for as they might be. Do these clues indicate that the houses are rented rather than owner occupied? Two of them display "For Sale" signs. We see young couples as well as elderly people. We notice a faded "home alert" sign in one window, then in another; apparently they have been there a long time. The entrances and windows do not have bars or grates. The sizes of the houses suggest that they were occupied originally by middle-income people, and the variety of architecture indicates that the area was built up over time, piece by piece, by a number of builder-developers. They seem to date from the 1920s and earlier.

Turning the corner onto San Fernando Street, we see more cars and traffic. One block north is Santa Clara Street, a wide street with heavy traffic and mostly auto-oriented commercial uses. It must be a main east–west street connecting with downtown San Jose. The houses on East San Fernando are not in as good condition as those on 16th or 17th, and yards are not as well maintained. One building houses a mental health advocacy project. We hear Spanish being spoken. Some young people are working on a car in the street. Does the commercial influence of Santa Clara Street continue down the side streets to East San Fernando? We think so, judging by the offices mixed with residences, the condition of some buildings, and the apparent income level of the people.

When we turn south on 15th street, the houses, apparently built in the 1920s and earlier, look better maintained than those on East San Fernando. There is a "For Sale" sign on one house. Next to it is an apartment building built in the 1950s or 1960s, judging by the stucco finish, lack of architectural detailing, alumi-

num casement windows, large plain surfaces, lower-quality materials, and less individual workmanship, compared to prewar construction. The people at this apartment house are white. We hear children's voices. At a similar apartment house we see some black people. Along the street a fair number of doors are open. There is a rooming house. Do the security stickers on doors and windows and the lace curtains indicate elderly residents? Some older people are walking on the street. Through one window we see a sculpture and books strewn casually about, suggesting younger people.

One house, originally a single-family, judging by its size and design, has been converted to five units; the five mailboxes were not originally part of the house. Students live there (a young black man dressed like a student in shorts and T-shirt, a street sign from France in a window). Another house has been converted to multiple units. Why were these older structures converted rather than replaced by higher-density buildings? Perhaps there was little demand for new housing at the time, or the area was relatively undesirable.

The sidewalks on 15th Street were repaved in 1966, according to the identification markings in them. In one house the sagging ground floor and a major crack in the center of the street facade indicate foundation problems.

East William Street seems to be a divider street: it is wide, has more traffic and fewer trees, and few of the houses face it or open on to it directly. On 14th Street between East William and East Reed, the houses are newer and better maintained than those to the north. This appears to be a more stable, maybe wealthier area. The houses on East Reed have alarm systems.

Homes on 13th Street, south of East William, are larger than on 14th. The parked cars are larger and more expensive than those we have seen earlier. A single-family home under construction looks expensive: board siding rather than plywood, a fair amount of nonstandard carpentry, variations in the facade, non-standard windows, and probably architect-designed. Many homes have electrical alarm systems, but front

doors are open. Because of the heat? There seems to be a mixed message here; the open front doors may be more significant than the alarms. We see few people on the sidewalks.

Still on 13th, but north of East William, the houses are older, smaller, and less well maintained. Is there a zoning change at East William, with more restrictions on the type of dwellings allowed to the south? We noticed similar changes in quality, size, and maintenance of the housing on three other north–south streets. On one house three doorbells indicate that what was originally a one-family has been converted to multiple units. Repair and maintenance work seems to have been done by nonprofessionals (uneven painting, paint lines that should have been straight but are not). Are young people moving in and doing their own rehabilitation work? We see younger people, some of Latin American origin. Three houses in a row have exterior metal window shades; probably a metal shade salesman came through the neighborhood in the late 1940s or early 1950s, when such shades were in fashion. Farther north on 13th we see evidence of more serious maintenance problems: cupped shingles, roofs in need of repair, missing and rotted materials, old and flaking paint. There is no danger of structural failure, only signs that people do not have enough money for proper maintenance, or that owners just are not doing it.

Moving north, we see a sign for a boarding house, a "For Sale" sign, a "For Rent" sign. More people are out on the streets, and more are Latin American. There are two homes for the mentally handicapped. A number of houses have external plumbing pipes, but we pay no particular attention to this. The last block of 13th, before Santa Clara, has a number of well-designed, older buildings, but the block has a transient feeling, as if the people are new or do not expect to remain a long time. Perhaps the outside pipes or the mix of uses or the institutions give it that feeling. A sign saying "Birth Home" indicates another social service. Why is it there—low rent? Nearness to clientele?

Paolo's Restaurant on Santa Clara looks as if it has

been there for a long time, and the parking lot, crowded with large and expensive cars, suggests that it draws customers from all over the city.

When we turn south on 11th Street, the first block, like other blocks immediately off Santa Clara, seems to be one of transition between the solid residential area to the south and the auto-oriented commercial uses on Santa Clara. The sizes of the homes tell us it was once solidly middle class. The San Jose Woman's Club here must have considered it an economically secure, family-oriented location. The street and its people have changed, we think. This is a one-way street, suggesting that the traffic is heavier here or that there is a perceived need to move faster.

The ATO Fraternity house at San Fernando reminds us that the university is nearby. A recent rehabilitation of this old Victorian is not well done; the materials and workmanship are not of high quality, and the painting is not crisp.

Large, old houses on 10th Street across from the university bespeak turn-of-the-century wealth. Later the original parcels were subdivided, and smaller houses built in between. The university owns much of the land and the buildings now, and, where it does not, the uses are oriented to it. University influence extends into the Naglee Park area on 11th, with a lot of university housing and many students. This is a heavily traveled one-way street.

Walking east on East San Carlos Street back toward the starting point, we see and smell flowers. The streets throughout Naglee Park are clean. At 15th and San Carlos is a home for older, semi-retarded people. They are visible inside. We have seen a number of such homes in the area. Why are they here? One of us recalls that in the early 1970s, the state's policies for care of the retarded favored housing them in small group homes in the community rather than in large institutions. The people were sent or otherwise moved to the larger cities: San Francisco, Oakland, San Jose. The care homes had to be in locations where prices were low enough and where the city would grant approval. The many care homes in the northern part of Naglee Park suggest that in the early 1970s house prices there were low and that there was no strong neighborhood association at that time. Neighborhood associations, which are usually organized in areas of good-sized single-family homes, tend to have strong misgivings about care homes. Perhaps a neighborhood group did object but was not strong enough to keep the care homes out.

Thinking about Naglee Park as a whole, we conclude that urban development started around the turn of the century. Very few buildings look older than this, and few are of the Bay Area early Victorian type. Development continued steadily but slowly. The many house designs and sizes, with not many identical houses in a row, tell us there were many small builders rather than one or two major developers. A few of the early homes were built for wealthy people, but by and large this seems to have been a middle-class area, judging by house sizes and the good but modest materials and designs.

The area south of East William was probably developed later than the area to the north; the houses look newer and a bit wealthier, with one exception: the quality of the housing along 11th is not as high as on the other streets south of East William. A zoning change may have been made along the rear property line between 11th and 12th, either confirming already existing differences or helping to create the differences.

We think that people started to move out of the Naglee Park neighborhood during the 1950s and 1960s to more desirable, newer, ranch homes in the suburban subdivisions. At that time the northern parts of this area may not have been particularly fashionable or desirable. At some point the area north of East William may have been rezoned for multifamily use (before that it was zoned for single-family use, if it was zoned at all). But since the 1960s change appears to have been slow: only a few new multifamily buildings and a fair number of conversions of older, single-family homes. Renters probably moved in during the 1950s and 1960s, including moderate-income Latin Americans. Homes were converted to rooming houses in the

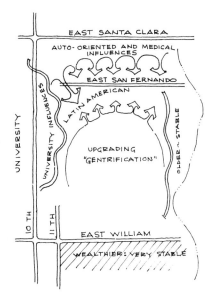

late 1960s or early 1970s, a little before the time when many houses became care homes for the mentally handicapped. Many owners, old and new, stayed on, however.

At present, a number of economic and demographic forces appear to be at work in Naglee Park. The commercial activities along Santa Clara push into the area from the north, and most of the north–south streets between Santa Clara and San Fernando appear to be a transition zone—some offices, parking lots or vacant lots, houses converted to boarding houses, care homes or social institutions, residential uses hanging on, with varying degrees of strength. From the west the university's influence is felt in student and perhaps faculty demand for housing, in the university housing on 11th, and in the cars parked near the campus. The Latin American influence seems strongest in the northwest corner of this neighboorhood, pushing toward the southeast. All of these influences seem to move toward a dividing line at East William, south of which are wealthier residents and moderately well-to-do homes, especially along 16th and 17th streets. Gentrification on a modest scale may be happening along 17th, pushing toward the northwest. Younger people, with children, are moving into the area, but a lot of older residents remain.

It seems a good bet that some people are having (or have had) second thoughts about the multifamily zoning, if that did in fact take place. The new people moving in probably will want the area to be as it had been originally, so zoning may be a subject of contention in the future. Does the present zoning make the new residents unsure about the future of Naglee Park?

The number of "For Sale" and "For Rent" signs, along with the presence of rooming houses suggests a high rate of turnover. Why? Are older residents dying, or are they moving out because the houses are too big and hard to maintain? Are recent buyers realizing significant profits by selling now? This last seems a bit doubtful, because those kinds of buyers might not be too interested in speculative profits.

Generally, the houses are well built and well maintained, although some have foundation problems and some could use better care. If the zoning north of East William is multifamily residential, it is not likely that replacement housing will be of as high quality in terms of materials and space per living unit as what now exists. Some people will want to change back to single-family zoning; others may argue that such a change would push out the less affluent ethnic groups who depend on this area for housing. All in all, Naglee Park is a fairly dynamic area, with a number of competing forces and interests. It is hard to tell now which will prove dominant. Will there be winners and losers?

The staff of the San Jose City Planning Department confirmed most of our observations and hypotheses, but they also pointed out at least one major misconception. Zoning has indeed been an issue in Naglee Park. Prior to 1951 the area was zoned for single-family dwellings. Attempts to allow multifamily development started in the 1940s, but it was not until 1958 that an alliance of property owners succeeded in getting the change made. Many of these owners were long-time residents, middle-aged and elderly, who were leaving the neighborhood and felt they could get better prices for their properties with more permissive, denser zoning. The city council at the time was very pro-development and agreed. People had started to move out of the area after World War II; some of the earliest residents had died, and structures were getting older and less up to date. The downtown area nearby was declining, as were many downtowns at the time. In short, the area was becoming less desirable. In the 1950s and 1960s Naglee Park slowly deteriorated. It was "redlined" by the banks, making it difficult for buyers to get property loans.[2] There were more conversions to multifamily use rather than new building of apartments in this period, attesting to an expanding market for student housing but not for new units in a somewhat declining neighborhood.

Up until 1968 students had to live either on campus or in university-approved boarding houses, which were concentrated on 10th, 11th, 12th, and 13th streets. A change in university policy in 1968 allowed students to live where they wanted, and many dispersed into the wider surrounding area. At the same time, as a result of the change in state policy on mental health care, approximately 70 percent of the county's board and care homes for retarded people moved into this neighborhood, where rents and prices were low. Less affluent and minority tenants also moved in during the period.

In 1973 the neighborhood association convinced the city not to deposit money in a particular bank until the bank stopped redlining. When the city withheld its deposits, the bank did change its policy and began giving housing loans again. Young professionals with families have been moving into the southern and eastern parts of the area since the early 1970s, as we surmised. At the end of that decade new buyers were concentrating on the northern and western parts of the neighborhood. The typical Naglee Park buyer in the 1980s is a married couple under forty and with a child. According to newspaper articles and the staff of the San Jose Planning Department, buyers are looking for houses with unique architectural features. As we thought, many new owners do their own improvements.

The Campus Community Improvement Association, the neighborhood group, has emerged as one of the strongest in the city. According to one source, they did protest the concentration of board and care homes in the early 1970s. In 1978 neighborhood residents succeeded in getting the zoning changed back to single-family, a policy that will prohibit further conversions to multifamily units and will prevent more board and care homes from coming into the neighborhood. An October 1981 newspaper article speaks of the newer home buyers becoming protective of the area.

Our observation that many of the residents are elderly was correct. The home alert stickers we saw were indeed from an older program. Recently, students have tended to move out of, rather than into, the area, according to Planning Department staff. Landlords prefer permanent tenants to nine-month student tenants. Field observations about a change in the zoning at East William and along 11th were correct.

The Planning Department staff confirmed our field perceptions of population dynamics in Naglee Park.[3] The area closest to the park has always been the more desirable, higher-income area, and 17th Street, along the creek, has always been a "good" area, known at one time as Doctor's Row. Block statistics from the 1980 census generally confirm that people with Spanish surnames are living in the north and west, though the area as a whole is basically a white enclave. The population includes both home owners and renters.

Santa Clara Street, which is historically significant as a segment of the original Camino Real, is a major entrance to downtown San Jose.[4] The Planning Department would like to keep the first block south of Santa Clara oriented to the immediate neighborhood. New development in that block is residentially related, they say. We question that. The medical offices have existed for a long time. The most recent nonresidential use, the birth center, was established around 1978. In order to maintain the residential nature of the area, the northern limit of the 1978 lower-density rezoning was in the first block south of Santa Clara. The staff contends that there is as much of a residential push northward as a nonresidential push southward. In that respect, then, our field diagnosis may not have been correct.

Perhaps a more significant misperception in our field observation concerned gentrification. Higher-income people are already moving in, and many households have two wage earners, according to the staff. Properties are being improved, sometimes by the owners, but the results do not yet show. Some of the inexpert workmanship we observed might be the result of landlords or tenants making minimal or make-do repairs. All of the rehabilitation in the area is privately funded, without the help of any government programs. Property values have risen sharply since 1975. The Planning Department considered the large number of "For Sale" signs a temporary phenomenon, generally on homes of residents who have died or elderly people who can no longer live alone. Conversions are to single-family from multifamily, not vice versa.

In sum, our field observations and diagnoses were

largely correct, particularly in regard to the history of development, the changes that have taken place, current population characteristics and dynamics, and the types of issues that are important in the neighborhood. Most of the conclusions we drew from observed details — signs, house stickers, people's ages — were also accurate.

On the other hand, we did not perceive accurately the pace of gentrification, the rezoning that had already taken place, and the strong community organization. Probably we were so pleased with our observation that zoning had been an issue and that one zoning change had already taken place that we failed to think through the second possible stage of change. Some evidence was there to interpret, if we had heeded it: no recent multifamily units, no evidence of new conversions, no new care homes.

Finally, it was confirmed that Paolo's is one of the oldest, best-known restaurants in San Jose and that it does serve a citywide clientele.

Almost immediately upon arriving in Naglee Park, we saw a parking sign on a residential street that limited cars without permits to parking during specific hours for nine months of the year. We put that clue with another, the nearness of the university, and some general knowledge of university schedules and student-faculty-staff driving habits. We concluded, tentatively, that university parking might be an issue for local residents. That relatively simple example contains many of the elements that make up field observation and diagnosis. The parking example and the Naglee Park case show what kinds of messages can be read in looking at urban environments.

We relate each visual clue to other clues and to the considerable knowledge and personal values that we bring to the situation. Some of the clues form patterns. All that we see contributes to a process, only partly conscious, of continual, rapid sifting of knowledge, recalling, forming conclusions, perhaps unknowingly, and of questioning what we see. I want to speak briefly of these matters before discussing the clues in detail.

The clues we recorded in Naglee Park were on a wide range of scale, from doorbells to the location of the area within the city of San Jose. Mostly, though, we used and reused five or six types of clues. Buildings were the most important indicators, and age, size, quality of materials, nature of design, and quality of maintenance were the most important attributes, along with yard maintenance and landscaping. The uses and the mix of uses and buildings were clues; for example, the mix of single-family and multifamily buildings in the center of the area helped explain some of its socio-economic dynamics over the years. Then there were single-purpose buildings, like the women's club or the Birth Home, that told us of the past and the present. People were very important clues, particularly their age, sex, race, ethnicity, and dress. The many small-scale indicators — doorbells, telephone wires, mail-boxes, and parking, "For Sale," and business signs, as well as toys, alarm systems, curtains, furniture, and even open doors — can be as important as the larger clues. Other cases provide different clues, but the ones we used in this small part of San Jose provide us with a good start.

Taken by themselves, however, individual clues mean very little. A modest-sized single-family house, even if we know that "modest size" means some 1,500 square feet, is, by itself, not much more than a single-family house. An older white man is an older white man. A single clue cannot give answers to the questions at hand nor permit conclusions about current and future issues. Usually we needed to combine clues, as in our university parking example, to gain an under-standing of the past and present dynamics of Naglee Park. Patterns, and breaks in the patterns, such as the differences north and south of East William, were important indicators of differences between areas or of changes that may be taking place. A break in a pattern brings up questions of why and when and what it might mean for the future.

As observers, we came to Naglee Park with consider-able general knowledge that helped us decode what we saw. We knew, from other cities, something about parking habits and issues, which made us aware that the type of parking sign was not altogether usual for a quiet residential street. From this we concluded that parking might be a problem. Knowing the general trends of urban residential areas following World War II allowed us to put together the conversion and market picture that evolved in Naglee Park during the 1950s and 1960s. Knowing about the shift in state policy on mental institutions told us why there are so many homes for the mentally handicapped in the neighborhood and helped us understand what that might mean about the housing market at the time. It is true that this kind of knowledge goes well beyond a general understanding of the history of urban development in America. But we all have more knowledge than we think we do, and observation that involves a conscious attempt to identify patterns and question what we see heightens the ability to recall what we know.

In the process of observation, it is extremely important to constantly question what one sees as well as the conclusions one comes to. Quite often in the description of Naglee Park, I have stated conclusions as if they were facts. What the eye sees is processed by the mind so speedily and unconsciously that the observer arrives at a conclusion without being aware of what generated it. In the field, for example, we observed that someone's "belongings seem not very substantial." Later one might ask what led to that conclusion, but at a conscious level the conclusions often come first. There may be no avoiding this. It is an example of how one's personal values and knowledge, whether or not they are appropriate to the situation, are brought into the act of observation. It is necessary to constantly question and refine one's definition of what is really being seen.

It is noteworthy that we began to reach tentative conclusions quite early in our walk; we did not wait until all the "facts" were assembled and sifted. The idea that Naglee Park was being upgraded and gentrified came early, based on very little evidence. Such "conclusions" should be treated as hypotheses while one is in the field and should be checked, tested, developed, and refined. In Naglee Park we should have been more open to new clues suggesting that much of the area had already been rezoned to permit only lower-density development.

The continual questioning and challenging of ideas, conclusions, and "light bulb" hypotheses is more likely to happen if there are two observers than one. A second observer can question the first and can add knowledge and see things that the other person does not. Two people's conclusions, however tentative, are based on more "data" and more experience than one observer's.

3 Clues

"The development consisted of imitation Tudor houses clustered along little concrete-and-grass pedestrian lanes. The place was doubtless designed for families with young children: traffic and parking lanes were safely isolated and almost every house seemed to have a tricycle or some form of hobby horse overturned on the lawn."[1]

What things that we see tell us what we want to know about urban areas: what are the clues? A clue or indicator is something that can be seen that tells the observer something he or she desires to know. Clues help the observer understand the nature of the urban environment being examined. They help answer some of the questions about the past, the evolution, and the present state of an urban area.

The meanings of some clues are obvious. A building with a 1920 date on it and four doorbells, four mailboxes, four light meters, and four telephone wires leading to it is obviously a four-dwelling-unit structure of known age. If the building was obviously designed as a single-family house and is surrounded by similar single-family houses, then it has obviously been converted: change has occurred. If construction workers up the street say they are converting other buildings, more change is on the way. Some obvious clues can be important: roofs with holes but with people living underneath, a wall that is seriously out of plumb, a sign announcing that a freeway is planned for the area. Such clues provide a basis for pursuing the more subtle clues, many of which are not obvious.

In thinking about clues there is no way to avoid categories and classification. The categories used here are ordered according to importance—that is, visibility and frequency—and according to sequence, the order in which one is likely to see them in the field. This kind of categorization has difficulties, because the eye and mind respond to what is there, not to preconceived categories or sequences. With that crucial qualification, we can proceed to consider the various kinds of clues: the things we see that tell us.

Buildings

Buildings are clues to so many of the things that people concerned with urban environments want to know. They are basic indicators of when development took place, its pace, and the nature and pace of activities in the area. They can also tell us who the area was originally intended for, as well as who lives in or uses it now, what changes have taken place over time, and how vulnerable the area is to change in the future. However, buildings is too broad a category to deal with; we need to consider specific characteristics. And sometimes groups of characteristics and groups of buildings, rather than individual elements are most significant.

Architectural Style

A building's architectural style is a major clue to when it—and perhaps the area—was built. This is true regardless of the building's function. Of course, the observer has to know when a particular architectural style was used—for example, that concrete apartment buildings with very little detail were not built until after World War II or that Victorian was before the turn of the century. Often, however, people with little or no formal knowledge of style can estimate, based on design, the age of buildings. A street with buildings all in the same style was probably developed at one time; a variety of styles usually means development over time by more than one builder.

But architectural style is not always revealing. Some styles were built over long periods; for example, the Georgian colonial style was built over a span of 180 years, up to the late 1700s. And style periods may overlap. A house in the bungalow style, which started in the late 1800s and persisted until World War II might have been built before a Victorian, whose style period ended at the turn of the century.

Then, too, builders are not bound by academic determinations of period; Georgian colonial houses are built in the 1980s. Usually there are clues one can use along with style, such as window details on a new Georgian colonial that are not the same as one would find on a 1750 Georgian, or contemporary joinery, or the absence of weathering, which make it easier to see the distinction between old-old and new-old. It is more difficult, however, to tell with certainty whether the buildings one sees are the original development in the area. Knowing architectural styles, particularly in an area where disparate periods are represented, helps the observer figure out what existed before the present development. It is not always certain that the newest buildings have replaced the earliest ones, or even that the oldest existing buildings were the first to be built. Fortunately, architectural style is not the only clue to when urban development took place.

Purpose

Houses, stores, factories, churches, offices, and schools usually have distinct physical characteristics that indicate their intended use. However, the more specifically one tries to categorize purpose as shown by building design, the more likelihood there is of error. In some periods and some countries, distinctions between house, school, and office are not emphasized. In Brazilia it is difficult, at first glance, to tell the difference between office buildings and certain apartment blocks. The exterior distinction between a contemporary office

and an industrial building is minimal in many cases. In the Baroque period the building facade was more important as a unifying design element than as an expression of intended use. But usually the design of the buildings in an area tell us their intended use and, by extension, the nature of activities in the area and who it was built for. If we compare the intended use of a building, according to its design, with the building's present use, we can begin to think about changes that have taken place.

Size

The sizes of buildings and of the units within them can be strong indicators of who an area was built for and who its present occupants are. In combination with other clues, building and unit size can help tell the history of an area's development, including life style values of the community, its economic structure over time, and something about local regulations.

Building size is important because of the direct correlation between size of building or unit and wealth of the occupant as well as the number and size of occupants. Because this is a broad assumption, it is important to take it cautiously, with qualifiers always at hand. Generally, smaller units are built for and occupied by lower-income people or activities and smaller families or businesses than are larger units. Put another way, people build or rent as much space as they need and can pay for. A large family lives in a small space only if they can't afford anything larger. When we see large houses or units, we assume they were built for people with more money. Other clues may support, modify, or question the premise, but that is the starting point.

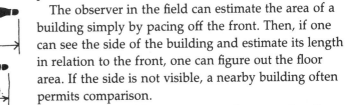

The observer in the field can estimate the area of a building simply by pacing off the front. Then, if one can see the side of the building and estimate its length in relation to the front, one can figure out the floor area. If the side is not visible, a nearby building often permits comparison.

In any country, for most types of construction floor-to-floor heights are remarkably uniform. It is easy to

make adjustments for nonstandard story heights once you know the norm.

The sizes of units within buildings can be more difficult to estimate. One way to begin is to divide the total area by the number of units, as indicated by the number of doorbells and mailboxes. This method does not account for different unit sizes, of course. A closer examination of the building may suggest where the interior partitions are, where one unit stops and another begins, thus permitting finer estimates of unit sizes.

But what do we mean by big and small? Measuring the size is fairly easy, but deciding on whether something is big or small or medium-sized is another matter. Like the standards of building condition, size is particularly laden with personal values. What is considered large or small often depends on cultural tradition, sometimes standardized by community regulation.

Nations, communities, and institutions have developed space standards as benchmarks for minimum acceptable housing quality. All countries that have publicly built and supported housing set standards for the number of rooms per dwelling unit, sizes of rooms, or space per person or family. Anything below the adopted figures is considered low, small, crowded, or substandard. During the 1960s India's Prime Minister Jawaharlal Nehru said that two rooms was to be the minimum size for housing in that country. The new standard sent planners, who had been working on a gross space standard, back to the drawing boards and reduced the size of individual rooms in new housing. In the United States, more than one person per room has been an indicator of crowding for many years. In America the Federal Housing Administration has used minimum room size standards as a basis for insuring loans since the 1930s. If one knows what the standards were when a building was constructed, one has some basis for saying that the building or unit is small or large.

But there are more satisfactory ways of coming to conclusions about size. If one knows what the common building practices were in the community at the time of construction, it is not difficult to say that the units are large or small. This approach, too, takes some prior knowledge, but it may be more useful to work from a norm rather than from arbitrary minimum standards. Knowing how buildings in the community are usually laid out gives an idea of how many bedrooms there are in a unit. From that, one can guess the number of people and the family type it was intended for. There are always exceptions—units with many bedrooms and no children, units with few bedrooms and many children. But we want only to determine the intended use of the building and the kinds of people who used to live in and now live in the neighborhood.

Failing all else, particularly if the observer is not familiar with community standards and common practice, there is another way to determine relative size: using one's own experience as the benchmark. We all know our own and our family's income level, living arrangement, rent, and space, and we remember what these variables were at other stages of life. That knowledge, used with caution, becomes the basis of comparisons with what is being observed and allows one to draw tentative conclusions about size.

Building size is one of those clues that, combined with others, can help one understand the history and present conditions of an urban area and even of the city as a whole. Consider size in combination with the quality of construction materials. If a small house or other building is of relatively simple, standard construction, we conclude that the original owner was less affluent than the owner of a similar building constructed of more specialized and higher-quality materials.

If house size is an indication of the income level and family size for which the area was originally built, then observations about the present residents can suggest how the area has changed. If small units are still occupied by low-income people, this suggests a certain stability. But if those units are now occupied by more affluent people, then the area may be more desirable than it was, or there may be a housing shortage in the city. Consider the Victorian houses on the southern slopes of Pacific Heights in San Francisco. The modest size of the houses suggests that the original residents were middle-income families. In 1983 that area was very expensive, and higher-income people, most without children, lived there, often in subdivided units. Conversely, if large houses have been subdivided and are now occupied by lower-income people, we guess that the neighborhood has become less desirable. Or the market for housing throughout the city may have changed, as happened for a period in Naglee Park. Now that neighborhood seems to be changing back to single-family housing. By understanding what was and comparing it with what is, we begin to understand change.

A situation that may be less obvious is that of large, old houses on spacious lots near the center of a city, once associated with great wealth but presently occupied by less affluent people. Such houses are often vulnerable to declining maintenance, to subdivision, and to replacement. Many visible clues — location in the city, age, quality of design and original materials, number of occupants, and maintenance — may lead one to suspect vulnerability, but *size* is the variable that triggers questions and further observation.

Size can be an indication of vulnerability in other ways. Both ceiling height and room area have a direct relationship to maintenance costs. It takes almost 40 percent more paint, to say nothing of labor costs, to cover a room ten feet by ten feet with twelve-foot ceilings than to cover such a room with eight-foot ceilings. A resident with limited income will paint and otherwise maintain a large unit less well and less often than a small one. A large unit occupied by low-income people is more vulnerable to poor maintenance. Size, then, can be a clue to vulnerability to change.

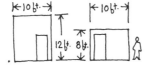

The relative sizes of nonresidential buildings can be a telling indicator of the economic makeup of a community. Size here refers to both height and bulk of a building as well as to the sizes of rented or owned units within it. These are indicators of the scale of entrepreneurship at the time of building, of changes that have occurred, and of anticipated markets for space. Consider Chestnut Street in San Francisco, where the commercial buildings are mostly one- and two-story structures. We will call that height low. Building widths

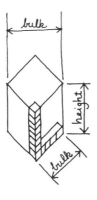

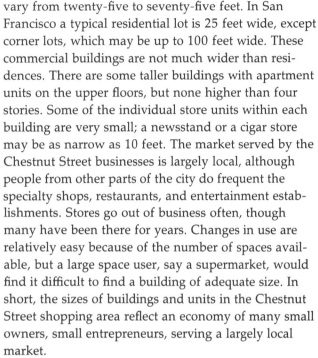

vary from twenty-five to seventy-five feet. In San Francisco a typical residential lot is 25 feet wide, except corner lots, which may be up to 100 feet wide. These commercial buildings are not much wider than residences. There are some taller buildings with apartment units on the upper floors, but none higher than four stories. Some of the individual store units within each building are very small; a newsstand or a cigar store may be as narrow as 10 feet. The market served by the Chestnut Street businesses is largely local, although people from other parts of the city do frequent the specialty shops, restaurants, and entertainment establishments. Stores go out of business often, though many have been there for years. Changes in use are relatively easy because of the number of spaces available, but a large space user, say a supermarket, would find it difficult to find a building of adequate size. In short, the sizes of buildings and units in the Chestnut Street shopping area reflect an economy of many small owners, small entrepreneurs, serving a largely local market.

It is possible that the many buildings were built by only a few owners, and it is possible that they are now owned by a few people and simply rented to many tenants. Various economic structures could exist in this physical setting, but the one described is the most likely.

Much of downtown San Francisco was at one time not all that different from Chestnut Street. The buildings, some of which still stand, were only slightly larger in height and width. Although the downtown area was much larger than the Chestnut Street area, suggesting a larger market area being served, one might come to similar conclusions regarding many small owners, entrepreneurs and developers. There were always some larger downtown buildings, and as time passed, some buildings were significantly taller and wider and had larger tenants than those of the original development. A view of the downtown at any given moment would show this shift in scale, suggesting a shift in ownership patterns and the nature of economic activity in the city, a shift from small to large.

The size of buildings today in downtown San Fran-

cisco reflects the presence of corporate headquarters, large-scale owners and developers, fewer individual entrepreneurs. Large developments suggest an anticipated market for the space. The developer-owners may satisfy a perceived need for diversity, particularly for retail and service functions, by including small shops at ground level, usually under tight design controls that are obvious to the observer. San Francisco's downtown, then, started small, physically and economically, but it has changed in scale, and the changes are visible.[2]

The messages of industrial buildings are similar to those of commercial buildings. Smaller units indicate smaller-scale operations with fewer employees. At the extreme, one large industrial building in a city suggests that the occupying industry dominates the economic life of the community.

Building size can also indicate certain standards or regulations that a community has adopted, telling us about some issues that have been and are important to its members. Height is a good example, usually in the form of maximum height allowed. The results of such regulations are often visible: no private buildings over a certain height in central Rome, as in many other European cities; large areas of one- and two-story buildings, except for taller ones at intersections, in some American cities; abrupt changes in height from one area to another. Buildings of the same height over an extensive

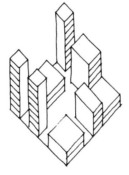

area are not usually the result of coincidence. A change in height regulations can be seen when all of the buildings built before a certain date are of one height while those built later are higher or lower. One building that is much taller than the others around it, even newer ones, may raise the question, why? And why not others? The Fontana Apartments at San Francisco's waterfront are an example. The answer may be that one person changed an unwritten norm—low height at the water's edge—and that afterward building height became an issue, resulting in a regulation on permissible height. Older, lower buildings amid newer, higher ones might reflect a concern for saving older buildings that was later expressed in a regulation to keep them. Most height regulations are associated with the cultural or design values of a community. Others have to do with building materials and standards for their use; for example, wood structures are permitted to rise forty feet above a concrete base in San Francisco, with other maximum heights for steel or reinforced concrete.

The overall size of a building may be controlled by a regulation on the amount of floor space that can be built in the area, presumably because of traffic and demands on public services and utilities. Such regulations are more difficult to see in the field because of variations in height, bulk, and area coverage. But the resulting mass or cubage of the building can often be read by a practiced eye. There are any number of other public controls on building size.[3] One recognizes them when one sees many buildings of the same general size though of different designs and ages or when one observes abrupt changes in size from area to area. Then, as always, one asks why.

Building size, then, is an important clue in understanding history, change, community issues or values, and vulnerability. It is also a strong indicator of the bargaining power of the people who built and of those who occupy the building.

Materials and Workmanship

It is easy to see what a building is made of on the outside, and we can often guess at what the interior materials are. The materials we can see, plus some knowledge of their quality, can help tell us who the building was built for, what materials were in style at the time of construction, whether the building will last, with or without major maintenance, and how susceptible it is to change. Again, the starting premise is economic: high-quality materials are generally expensive, so people with wealth are more likely to build and occupy buildings in which such materials are used.

It is important to understand what influence local characteristics—say a very cold or a wet climate—have on the materials used. I will not try to list all of the possible situations or to catalogue materials and their relative qualities, let alone construction methods. But the observer should be aware of the types of situational variables. These include geographic location (brick is not a high-quality material in an earthquake-prone area such as Tangshan, China); availability of materials (wood is no longer available in Tangshan, and reinforced concrete can be used only if reinforcing steel is available); availability of skills (people who can lay brick and engineers who can show how to build low, safe, brick buildings). Familiarity with the properties of various materials helps one understand why a particular material has been used. And the materials used can help one understand the situation. The use of scarce materials may be a sign of wealth or prestige or importance.

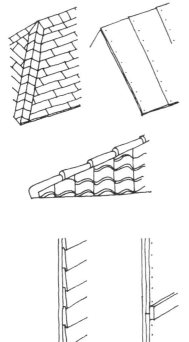

But what is the meaning of quality in materials? Solid one-inch plank siding is a higher-quality material than plywood or shingles, but the definition depends on the circumstance. A tarpaper roof might be just as adequate as tile for a temporary building or a storage shed in a moderate climate where it seldom rains. An imprecise but useful working definition of adequate material quality is durability and suitability for the intended job without undue maintenance or replacement. A tarpaper roof is not a high-quality material in cold, windy Chicago; seeing such a roof in that city tells us that the people living under it are probably poor.

Interestingly, observers without much formal knowledge of building materials can often tell the difference

between high and low grades. Thin stucco somehow looks different from thick stucco, even when you cannot see the thickness: a high-grade exterior plywood looks different from a lower grade. Generally it is not difficult to make the connection between materials and the economic status of the people for whom they were intended. Gauging workmanship is a bit more difficult, requiring some knowledge of how buildings should be constructed. A good starting point is to ask whether elements that ought to be straight really are and whether pieces join tightly. Again it is not difficult to identify the extremes of low-quality and high-quality work.

For city planners, the major concern in quality of materials and workmanship is not so much who the building was intended for or who uses it now, but its durability. Triple-layered slate shingles, usually considered a high-quality roofing material, are costly to maintain when they get old. The quality of materials in relation to the occupiers' ability to maintain them, can indicate vulnerability to rapid change. If people of moderate incomes fall on hard times, they find it difficult to maintain a lower-quality, high maintenance building. Building or neighborhood decline and decreased property valves could then take place.

Many professionals with middle-class values tend to look down on materials of lesser quality than we are accustomed to, to assume that they are not likely to last. That is part of a mental process that has resulted, I think, in many of the decisions to tear down areas of cities. The buildings may be sound when the decision is made, but it is assumed that they soon will be slums.[4] So one should be very cautious about concluding that materials are of less than adequate quality.

Design Quality

It can be argued that everything made by man is designed. But in urban environments a "designed" building or complex usually means one that stands apart; concentrated effort went into its design. It may be unique in appearance, or complex in details and arrangements, or different from "standard," or created by a "designer." I am not referring to good or bad design or just to buildings designed by architects.

It is usually not difficult to distinguish an urban structure that has been "designed" from those that are standard or for which no special design effort was made. This also applies to a large complex of buildings or distinctive tract of housing, even though each building within the complex is similar.

What might the presence of carefully designed structures in an urban area imply? Usually greater economic resources have been spent on a designed building, so the builder must have had those resources. Of course part of a building's specialness may be that it is smaller than "usual" and therefore less costly, implying that the owner-renter has less money than his neighbors. In any case, though, the initiators of the design probably had a sense of values, aesthetic or otherwise, that were different from their neighbors', or they may simply want to attract attention.

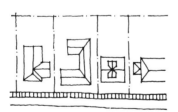

To see what specially designed buildings can tell us, it is worth turning to some specific situations. On some city streets every building is different, and each one seems to have been individually designed. It is reasonable to conclude that they were all built for people with higher incomes than those who occupy more standard buildings. If they are all well maintained, then one can conclude that the present occupants are also well to do. One or two new individually designed houses in an area of older designed homes suggests that the area is stable and confidence that it will be maintained. On the other hand, the presence of standard, smaller houses or apartments in an area of older, individually designed buildings suggests there has been a shift in the income level of residents and in the

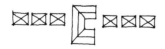

market for housing. Obviously, any number of combinations is possible.

What of large-scale tract housing such as the Levittowns in the east and the Eichler developments in California? Considerable design effort has gone into these developments. We can assume that the purpose was to save construction costs and lower sales prices, so that a large number of people could afford to buy.[5] The houses were often smaller than standard but were designed to make a better, more efficient use of the space. The developers were apparently concerned with economies of scale that can be achieved through special design and with more efficient design that would appeal to a mass market.

Housing has been the model for most of this discussion of design, but the same points apply to nonresidential buildings as well. Specialness involves greater cost, except when the specialness, often on a large scale, expresses the ''design'' of lowering costs.

Maintenance and Condition

More than the other clues we have considered, building maintenance is a clue to change and vulnerability to change. It can therefore tell us of the presence of—or need for—neighborhood policies and action programs. Maintenance and condition are clues to the residents' income levels and the value people put on their homes and neighborhoods. At the same time, maybe more than any other single characteristic, building maintenance and condition can be misread and used to justify inappropriate public actions.

When we look at a building, we see surfaces, materials, openings, connections, and details such as railings, gutters, or steps. Their condition shows how well the building has been maintained. Paint may have a healthy sheen, or it may look chalky or have bubbles or be flaking off. Walls that should be vertical may lean, and floors and roofs may no longer be horizontal. Roof shingles, instead of lying flat and even, may be cupped, and some may be missing. Check to see if replacement parts are thicker or thinner than the originals and of better or poorer quality. Window frames

should join tightly with wall surfaces; if they do not, there may be signs of leaks. Downspouts should connect with and slope toward continuous gutters, but some areas may have rusted away or loosened, permitting water to pour down the walls or along the foundation. Look for cracks or settling in the foundation. New siding materials, such as shingles or aluminum siding, should be butted tightly at corners and openings. Overall, one looks for precise workmanship, with tight joints and straight lines, or a more careless approach.

Building maintenance consists of many aspects, some very important, many not. Obviously, it helps to know something about building materials and to have a standard of adequate maintenance before inferring very much from looking at buildings. A large, bare-looking wall of wood siding, even with a few boards missing, may not be difficult or expensive to repair. In looking at building condition and maintenance one should always remember that very few buildings in a community fall down in any given year for *any* reason, let alone from lack of paint. Sagging floors and leaning walls do not usually mean the building will collapse tomorrow. It is important to know the difference between present and potential dangerous conditions. After repeated failures to find the source of a leak and fix it, more than one property owner has taken the advice of the genius who said, "Make friends with your leak." I do not wish to make light of building condition or its importance as a clue. But it should be kept in perspective.

One benchmark of condition and maintenance is whether the building has been kept at its original quality, taking into account normal aging and weathering of materials. That measure allows for the reality that buildings and whole neighborhoods start out at different quality levels. One should know not only what the original conditions were, but also something of building technology and maintenance and effect of the local climate on materials. Clearly, too, the general condition of buildings in an area is as important as that of individual structures.

Building owners, especially if they live on their

property, usually try to maintain them as well as they can afford. People usually buy and occupy houses they can afford, or that are only a bit beyond their economic means at the time of purchase. Usually, a well-maintained single-family house is assumed to be owner-occupied. If the maintenance is shoddy or poor, we wonder about the economic status of the owner and whether the occupants are renters rather than owners. Renters are less likely to be responsible for exterior maintenance of property, even if it is a single-family home, and the owners may not be able to keep up with repairs for any number of reasons. An excellently maintained modest-sized (two to ten units) apartment building may also suggest owner occupancy, particularly if one sees signs of personal touches in painting or repairs.

We assume too that renters desire to live in well-maintained housing and do so consistent with their means. Poor maintenance of multiple-unit buildings suggests that the income from tenant rents is not adequate to maintain the property or that the owner is permitting it to deteriorate in favor of higher profits — or both. In general, we assume a direct relationship between maintenance and income: as one goes up so does the other, and vice versa.

There are exceptions, of course. Among some cultures, exterior house maintenance is not so important; the insides of houses provide the clues. The people behind those unpainted, chipped, cracked walls may not be poor. And remember that building maintenance is not the only clue to the occupants; I have spoken of building size and will discuss other clues. Lack of maintenance may be a clue that public image is not important to the occupants or that their emphasis is on private life. It is important to distinguish between basic and superficial maintenance. Unpainted walls or cracked and chipped stucco may not be very important. Signs of seriously sagging floors or missing or rotting structural members are more telling. We need to take a closer look. Some other clues may suggest the incomes of the inhabitants: a nameplate, a bell, or a distinctive, polished brass doorknocker in striking contrast to the

gray, chipped walls; new or recently varnished window frames; or, conversely, rusty downspouts and crumbling walls. It may take some looking, but the clues are often there.

Judging the maintenance of nonresidential buildings is more complicated. The visual manifestations of good maintenance in a steel mill or factory are different from those in a house. Still, many of the signs of maintenance are similar for all buildings and uses. Since the 1960s light industrial buildings have been made increasingly to look like residences or small-scale office buildings. And employees and the community have come to expect neat, well-maintained buildings, particularly in so-called industrial parks. There is status in owning or working in an industrial building whose function is masked by its appearance. If an industry has a negative image in the community, design controls may try to overcome the unpleasant associations. Such buildings are often maintained as if they were homes. Signs of inadequate maintenance makes the observer question the economic well-being of the business or the developer. One has only to look at a development like the Ravenswood Industrial Park in East Palo Alto to know that it is not thriving.

Signs of good or poor maintenance may be harder to see in older industrial and warehouse buildings, particularly in older cities. There may be little reason to clean old brick walls covered with years of grime or to paint metal window casements or even to wash the windows. Such clues may have no relation to the economic soundness of the industry or the level of employment. Good structural conditions, where they can be seen — vertical walls and columns, floors without sag, tight roofs — may be much more important in gauging the industry's ability to withstand change. To judge, one needs some knowledge of the history of industrial development in urban areas, together with clues such as whether buildings are occupied and whether broken windows, for example, have been replaced. One can also try to ascertain whether the design and construction of the buildings are adaptable to changing societal requirements.

In a heavy industrial complex (a steel mill, a foundry) the most important maintenance clues may be found in the area that houses management. Administrative offices are more likely to resemble office or even residential construction, and the maintenance clues are similar.

In all of these cases the quality of maintenance indicates the financial capabilities of the owner or occupant, modified by personal or cultural values.

Changes from one area to another also may suggest some of the issues that may be present in the community. Imagine a turn-of-the-century neighborhood where the houses were constructed of the best possible materials and with the highest-quality workmanship. If the houses have always been maintained "just like new," this suggests a certain stability in the incomes of the occupants. If the relative costs of maintaining that quality have risen, we can infer that the present occupants are even wealthier than the original owners.[6] Buildings whose original construction and materials were of low quality and have remained in their original condition also indicate stability. Better maintenance than in the past and higher-quality replacement materials suggest upgrading, either by owners with higher incomes or through a government program. An area of lower-quality homes next to a better residential area is a good place to look for upgrading. If the people in the lower-quality area cannot pay for improvements, they may be displaced by economic pressures or even by government programs that mandate improvements. This process of gentrification is very difficult to chart statistically, but it can often be predicted for an area by astute observation.[7]

Change can go in many directions, depending on a number of variables. Good maintenance in an area, together with recent construction and few vacancies, suggests a strong market for housing. Widespread maintenance efforts in one particular time period could indicate that the community sponsored or required improvements. A uniform look could mean that a good salesman of a new product, such as permastone, came through the neighborhood at just the right time. A strong indication of public funding is major rehabilitation, such as new roofs, stairs, siding, windows, and painting, in an area whose residents do not appear able to afford the work. Recent changes, which are usually easy to spot, should be weighed in relation to other variables to get a sense of the dynamics of an area. It is worth noting that an account of these kinds of changes is seldom available from other sources.

Land and Landscape

Like building maintenance, the treatment of yards and land can be an indicator of economic status, ethnic values, and other matters as well.[8] The observer can see how extensively outdoor residential space is used and by whom. Worn areas mean heavy use, perhaps by children or pets. Outdoor cooking arrangements suggest a particular life style, and slides and play equipment suggest children. A paved front yard suggests that easy maintenance is a prime consideration. Some people who do not place a high value on the land around their house may pave their yard or ignore it. But paving is a landscape decision, too. Four automatic sprinklers in a 100-square-foot grass plot suggest that the owners like the lawn but do not want to spend a lot of time hand watering it.

Generally, unusual trees and plants and professional landscaping are associated with higher incomes. But gardening is an activity that people of all incomes enjoy. The yard of a lower-income person can be as well landscaped and meticulously cared for as that of a wealthy person. Over many parcels, however, one expects income characteristics to prevail.

Many developers and managers of rental and condominium properties believe that intensive landscaping is a selling point, that well-cared-for grounds can justify higher rents. It sometimes pays to see whether the landscaping quality is equal to that of the buildings. If, in a new development, the landscaping is considerably better than the building quality, it would not be surprising if the landscaping deteriorated after the initial sales pitch was over.

Maintenance of land around public housing can be

heavy and dense trees and shrubs

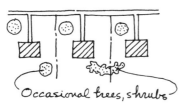

Occasional trees, shrubs

Communicating

Easy   Difficult   May Be Awkward

an indicator of its relative importance to the management, the financial state of the agency that runs it, and the attitudes of tenants to their homes. Landscape funds are usually one of the first things to be cut in a budget crisis, but there are examples to the contrary. In Cleveland, under the administration of Ernest Bohn, the design and maintenance of grounds of public housing projects were far better than for most private developments. Bohn believed that good landscaping was a relatively inexpensive way to enhance modest building design. During the 1950s it was common to see flowers and even vegetables, planted by tenants, around doorways in those housing developments. This suggests that the tenants had a positive relationship with management and each other and a good feeling about the development as a place to live. It is easy to list examples of disregard by management or tenants in public and private housing, and this too indicates people's feelings about where they live.

The kinds of landscape arrangements one sees in an area permit some hypotheses about communication and perhaps even about the likelihood of neighborhood action. Hedges, trees, and flower beds can be arranged so that communication between neighbors is either easy or difficult. Planting can facilitate communication or make it more awkward. From the nature and design of the landscape, we can guess whether people are likely to talk to each other regularly. *Likely* is the key word.

Use of Buildings and Land

We observe and take messages from the uses made of land and buildings so automatically that we may not be aware we are doing it or how important it is. Stores show us what we can purchase; hotels tell the traveler that lodging and food are available; the areas next to railroad yards are avoided by middle-income people in search of housing. We know these things without identifying the clues as land uses. Often a land use is not seen directly, but certain clues permit us to conclude that people work, buy and sell, or reside there. Or we can tell what the land use is directly: people buying and selling in a store or an outdoor market, children playing, signs that say what is happening on a site.

Land uses tell something of the *nature of activity* in an area. The size of the area indicates how many or few people do those things. The size, of a shopping center can suggest how large an area people come from to find what they want—that is, whether the center is locally or regionally oriented. If people come from a wide area, then one asks how they get there, and one thinks about traffic volume. Diversity of uses in an area, along with size, tells more.

A lack of some uses, too, is telling. If there are no stores in an area, or none of a particular kind, one wonders where people shop. Do they drive, or is there public transportation to shopping areas? If they take public transit, they cannot buy very much at one time. An absence of parks may mean that parks are not very important to the people in the area, or it may mean that there is a need for parks, but no available space, or that the government is not responding to need.

Land uses may be homogeneous over a large area—all housing, for example, even all single-family houses, or all commercial buildings, or a mixture.

The economic diversity or homogeneity of a metropolitan area or of one section of a city is usually visible. That visibility, combined with the observer's knowledge of economic development and location patterns, can permit some conclusions about an area's relative stability or vulnerability. An area of three-bedroom, one-family detached houses or of six-story apartment buildings with one- and two-bedroom units can accommodate many different kinds of people: such is the adaptability of space. But it is a good bet that such a homogeneous area was built with a particular population in mind, a limited range of possible occupants. If the present occupants are clearly different from the intended population, then we ask why. A single-use office area suggests a need for transportation for those who work there. We also can guess that there is little or no activity there during evenings or weekends. Some segment of the community is likely to express the

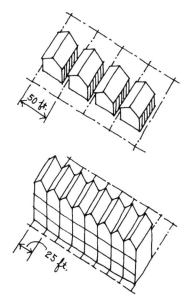

desire for more activities so that the area is "alive" throughout the week.

Obviously, there are endless possible combinations and arrangements of land uses and their implications in a given situation. What is important to understand is that the uses can be seen and that they constitute meaningful clues.

The relative *intensity* of a use, that is, the amount of activity on the piece of land, is usually visible. Population density is related to intensity. A low-density urban residential area, say with one dwelling unit on each 50-by-100-foot lot,[9] is visibly different from an area of buildings with three units on every 25-by-100-foot lot. Just seeing that much tells us that the first area will generate a smaller market for shops than the second, that transportation modes will be different, that public transit will be more economically feasible in the second, and more. Family sizes in the two examples might be the same, but the life styles of residents probably are not. The lower-density area has more land available to meet residents' needs and may require more care. Occupancy by owners is more likely with lower density. Residents of a higher-density area might have to, or want to, satisfy more recreation needs away from their homes than residents of a lower-density area. Life styles, then, will be different, either marginally or significantly.

Similarly, the visible intensities of nonresidential development suggest what needs exist for access, transportation, and services. Some needs will be apparent, for example, transit, parking, solutions to congestion, police, street cleaning.

Types of nonresidential uses are usually observable and can tell us something about the economic base of the community, about the area's relative stability. Pittsburgh's earlier emphasis on heavy industry — mills, factories, smoke — was always visible. Its present offices, banks, research institutions, and light industry suggest some diversification, but with a large dependence on the older, still visible, factories. The Oakland area of Pittsburgh is education, medical, and cultural

institutions. The businesses of the Fisherman's Wharf area of San Francisco depend on tourists, not fishing. The observable nonresidential uses in the Palo Alto area are related to electronics. Modesto, with its irrigation systems and farms has a visible agricultural base. Orvieto, Italy, is wine and ceramics.

The nature of nonresidential uses is a clue to the kinds of people who are likely to live nearby, in the city or immediate area. The electronic and computer firms of the San Francisco peninsula hire different people from those hired by the Ford Company in Detroit and from the people who work for the government in Washington, D.C. If we assume that people prefer to live near their work place if they can, we would expect local employment sources to indicate who lives nearby. Of course, some industries are less desirable as neighbors, and the less environmentally desirable an activity is, the more likely it is that people with enough money to do so will live farther away.

Changes in land use are also revealing. In Chapter 5 I deal more extensively with change as a phenomenon, but consider the following examples. Multifamily units in what used to be single-family houses indicate changes in the market for housing, in the nature of people who occupy the space, and in life styles; offices or stores in what were houses represent a significant shift; dwelling units in former industrial loft space indicates that the demand for housing is stronger than that for industry or storage; care homes in single-family houses suggest that the original owners wanted to leave the area, that they found it hard to sell to other people for the same use, and that there was no legal or community prohibition on the change of status.

Changes in land use and new uses can indicate existing or future problems. A new shopping center with the same kinds of stores as the existing stores in the adjacent area makes one question whether the market is expanding and whether both centers can survive. The construction of a major new commercial center has long been a visual indicator that the older downtown shopping district was or would soon be vulnerable to economic decline. In looking at new developments, one asks about the market for them and the likely effects on nearby similar land uses. This gives some idea of possible community issues.

I have just touched the surface of a large subject: what the visible uses of land and buildings can tell of the dynamics of an area. My intent is not to be all inclusive; the purpose is to look at land use as a major indicator of what has been, is now, and is likely to be happening in an urban area.

Special-Purpose Buildings

A residential, commercial, or industrial area is very rarely purely that. Somewhere in any of those areas one can find a church, a firehouse, a school, even a stadium. Most of these uses are public or semipublic, and often they stand out visually.

Such buildings often have dates on them, which can be a clue to the age of the surrounding development. Older public buildings help tell who the earlier development was for and who lives there presently: schools mean families with children; Catholic churches mean Catholic residents; Slovenian halls mean a Yugoslav community; fraternity houses are a signal of a university nearby. Stability or change may be apparent: a school may be as old as the houses and may still be in use, or it may be vacant or converted to another use, or it may be new; a church may have a new name or information in a different language; the firehouse may be closed. Such changes may be clues to a neighborhood's influence and its vulnerability to change, past and present: most people are happy to have a neighborhood library branch, but no one wants a stadium or sewage treatment plant. Town and gown issues come up anytime a university plans to expand; a small police station is expensive and may be uneconomical, but in a high crime area the residents may have pressed for a stronger police presence.

Artifacts

The details on buildings, which I will call artifacts, can be as telling as larger elements. Artifacts, usually utilitarian and often added to a structure by its occupants, can help to verify or refute an observer's hypotheses. The number and types of artifacts as clues are almost limitless. I will list and discuss briefly those I have found to be the most helpful indicators in the field.

Address identifications and house numbers can tell where the area is in relation to some starting point or to the city center. Usually street numbers get higher as one goes away from the center. The numbers can also indicate unanticipated changes that have occurred over time: a sequence is broken by half numbers or missing numbers; a sequence such as 456 followed by 456A means that a housing unit was added after the street was numbered.

The graphic style of house numbers may indicate the owner's personal style or a prevailing fashion. How clearly visible they are may show how much the residents want to aid people who are looking for the house. Or the style, location, visibility, and age of numbers may be the result of a local ruling. In a Cincinnati neighborhood where the houses varied in style and age, new helvetica-style numbers of uniform color and size were a clue to a recent community decision.

Mailboxes and doorbells often reveal the number of units in a building and permit the observer to estimate unit size by dividing the total square footage by the number of units. New mailboxes and bells indicate that units have been added. The accessibility of the mailbox and whether it is locked tells whether security is a concern.

Nameplates of occupants can indicate the ethnic composition of an area and where the territory of an ethnic group begins and ends. Students in San Francisco used this as one indicator of the boundaries of Chinatown. Nameplates are also a clue to some living arrangements, as when two or more surnames are given. Nameplates can identify the types of professions and businesses ("Hong Kong Import-Export Co." or "John Lewis, Attorney at Law") in a building or an area, including businesses in what appear to be residential buildings. A nameplate such as "The Andersons" suggests that the occupants are proud of their home and neighborhood. People who put their own

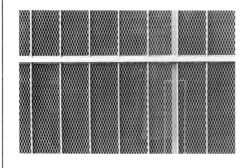

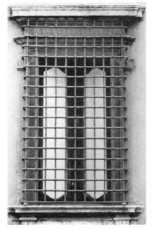

name on their home are decidedly not afraid to be identified. Vacation homes often seem to have names, such as "Sea Breezes."

Grates, grilles, alarm boxes, and home alert signs are age-old indicators of safety and crime issues as perceived by area residents. People go to the expense of placing those devices over windows and doors only if they perceive that crime is a problem. An observer should look for clusters and patterns of those devices—one street has them, another does not, a third has them at one corner and not another—and signs of how recent they are. These factors allow one to speculate about the location and urgency of the problem. In some areas window stickers indicate that the neighborhood has organized to confront the crime issue. "Beware of Dog" signs and fences are also indicators, as are television surveillance systems and floodlights.

But these clues can be misleading. Once a protection device is attached to a building, it probably will not be removed, even if the problem no longer exists. And the absence of such clues does not mean there is no crime problem. The residents may not be able to afford such devices or may find them repugnant, or there may be less visible crime deterrents at work, such as concentrated police patrols or private surveillance.

Lawn, balcony, and porch artifacts—toys, basketball hoops, bicycles, lawn furniture, cooking grills, lawn decorations, and clotheslines—tell a great deal about the people who live in an area. The age, quality, condition, and degree of permanence of such artifacts are all part of the picture. Toys, of course, indicate children, and the types of toys allow one to guess the ages. In America, bicycles on apartment balconies suggest teenagers or young adults and inadequate storage space. In upper-income neighborhoods in the United States, clotheslines are rarely seen. The clothes hanging on lines may bespeak the residents' type of work or life style. Given that most incidental artifacts are easily stolen if left unsecured, their presence is a clue that the residents are not greatly concerned about petty theft and vandalism.

In some geographic areas there seems to be a strong

relationship among social class, religion, and decorative artifacts.[10] Eagles, colonial lamp posts, rustic signs, and unique mailboxes are more often displayed by people whose social and economic status have recently risen than by "old money" families.

Automobiles can be misleading. Although it is easy to tell their size, age, make, relative value, condition, and maintenance, there are too many variables to allow one to relate those factors directly to types of owners. You don't have to be wealthy to drive a Cadillac, and some wealthy people drive small cars. One sees more standard-sized American cars in the Midwest than in San Francisco, where smaller imports are more common, but that does not tell us much about the Walnut Hills area of Cincinnati. But one can observe the number of cars in a residential area in relation to the number of housing units. Trucks and campers give some notion of life styles, and motorcycles are usually associated with young people. It is possible to see repair work being done on cars in yards and garages.

A building's windows may be clean, dirty, or somewhere in between. There may be good reason to read something into window condition, particularly in association with other indicators. But whether windows are regularly washed may be culturally determined or a matter of local habit more than anything else. In India windows are normally not very clean or seem to have been washed with dirty water. In Cork, Ireland, they shine, even in small, poor houses, but that is not the case in Dublin. In the United States clean, shiny windows seem to be the norm for middle- and upper-income areas but not usually for the very lowest-income areas, especially where the population is transient. We are less surprised by dirty windows when the buildings are in poor condition, when the units are very small, when a commercial use is economically marginal, when the street has heavy traffic, when an apartment building has many vacancies, or when the blinds or curtains behind them are makeshift. Men, except gay men, may be less likely to wash windows than women.

Window curtains and blinds are another story. A

middle-class mother is not likely to haphazardly hang an Indian madras bedspread over a window unless it is her first night in the house. Makeshift materials and methods of hanging are often indicative of lower-income people who do not feel settled in the neighborhood. Lower-income people cannot afford to hang delicate, thin-slatted venetian blinds. Young professionals are likely to use fashionable, designer fabric, maybe with the designer's name and label visible, on their windows. Materials, styles, and ways of hanging curtains and blinds, if they are hung at all, can tell something about an area's residents. Also, window coverings, once bought and hung, are not usually changed for a long time.

We hypothesize that stylish fabric, up-to-date blinds, and wood shutters are used by people concerned with fashion, people who may have moved into the units recently. Less fashionable fabrics and designs usually indicate older people of traditional values, and more modest means. Such clues can be tricky. In the past everyone "knew" that lace curtains, the kind that had to be dried on curtain stretchers with all those nails, were used by middle-class and lower-middle-class families. Synthetic fabrics and the cycles of fashion have made lace curtains fashionable again in the 1980s, so one can't always tell about the income level of the residents.

If window coverings are similar throughout an area, that might help confirm a hypothesis about social homogeneity. Distinct differences in style or quality of window coverings suggests a mixed population or perhaps new people moving in.

In a building with multiple units, checking the number of windows with identical curtains can help determine or confirm unit or room sizes. Sometimes, however, the occupant does not control what the observer sees from outside; the management may provide the drapes or dictate their color and other characteristics.

One can sometimes see furniture and other interior artifacts, which give the same messages by and large, as curtains. With a little knowledge of furniture, books,

artworks, and their arrangement, the observer can confirm ideas about the occupants' incomes, ages, and lifestyles.

Electric meters and water meters must be located where the meter reader has access to them, so sometimes they can be seen from the street. This is an easy way to tell how many units are in a building or to surmise who is paying for what. Some residential buildings in San Francisco's Chinatown have no visible bells or nameplates to indicate the number of occupants. But if one sees forty electric meters just inside a back door, then one knows the number of units and can guess at the number of people. It is also clear that light and heat are not included in the rent.

Telephone and electric wires leading to buildings are another clue to the number of units. If a number of telephone wires lead to a house that looks like a single-family, it is likely that the house has been subdivided into individual rooms for boarders or into business offices. In older areas the absence of overhead wires means that some group made an effort to have them placed underground, perhaps through a community or neighborhood campaign.

Bright street lights on a quiet residential street may indicate that the neighborhood has had a security problem—residents often demand better lighting in those situations—or that there has been a public works program to replace old lights. Well-maintained old lights or newly designed fixtures indicate that the community has put some special effort into street lighting.

Signs are among the most important clues in understanding an environment; their purpose is to inform, and little interpretation is necessary. Sometimes, though, the messages go beyond the words, numbers, or pictures. "For Rent" and "For Sale" signs are good examples. Not only do they tell what properties are on the market, they may make it clear that there is a high turnover of houses in the area. The condition of the sign—the word "Sold" slapped on a new sign, or an old, dirty "For Sale" sign—shows how fast the property is moving. If one knows how many units there are on a street and how often the residents tend to move, one can get a reasonable impression of whether five or six "For Sale" signs constitute a trend or an insignificant number.

Signs for drivers, such as child safety or parking-hour signs, can tell something about the neighborhood and its issues. Stop signs at every intersection may mean there have been traffic problems. Or, if there is very little traffic, they may just mean that a very effective neighborhood association has been concerned about cars speeding through. Tow-away signs, one-way signs, detour signs — they all tell about the nature of the traffic and how the community is dealing with it.

Public information signs and notices advise of many things beyond their literal messages: how active a community is, who is looking for what, who the residents are, and whether the area is oriented to local residents or to a larger community.

Graffiti usually signify the presence of teenagers. They may literally express some issues that concern those who did the writing, who often do not feel that they are part of the mainstream of the community.

Business signs also tell more than the immediate, direct message. A tattered banner sign is likely to indicate a poorly kept, cheap eating place rather than a well-kept, expensive one. Signs tell something about the age of the store, the clientele served, the economic status and values of the owner, whether ownership is local or not, and the presence or lack of community restrictions on size or type of signs. Signs indicate who the shopping area is for — men, women, a class of people.[11] The characteristics to look for are design style, condition and maintenance, materials, age, size, and, of course, the words or symbols used.

People

Psychologists and others advise us to be cautious in reaching conclusions about people just by looking at them. "The poor are persons who live in a certain section of town and not necessarily the people who wear the most tattered clothes . . . A prostitute is a woman standing alone in the Tenderloin and not necessarily a woman in a revealing costume."[12] Fair enough, but how does one identify the Tenderloin? Maybe, in part, by seeing a number of women standing alone, dressed in eye-catching, if not revealing, costumes. Observing people is useful in making hypotheses, some with certainty and some to speculate about with caution.

People's age, race, and sex are obvious indicators of who lives in or frequents an area. But it is possible to tell more. Clothing styles give one a notion of their interests, life styles, and economic status. Fashions change, but it is not difficult to distinguish expensive from inexpensive, or high fashion from conservative or office dress from blue-collar work clothes. Uniforms, whether formal like a policeman's or informal like a stockbroker's, tell what people do. At Diamond and 24th in San Francisco, women, middle-aged and older, were wearing simple wool coats with hats and black, comfortable, low-heeled shoes; their ages and styles suggest that the area residents have a middle-income, family-oriented life style. Along with other clues, the clothing and the grooming of the men at Castro and Market streets identify them as gay. Within that culture, knowing observers see other distinctions.

The needy, in one way or another, often show it. The presence of one mentally or physically handicapped person in an area may mean very little, but seeing many such people in one area suggests that they live or work nearby. Group homes or workshops may be needed and may be an issue in the neighborhood.

Commercial Areas

Both in their component parts and as distinct land-use concentrations, commercial areas are extremely important as sources of information. Such concentrations of clues and activities more fully represent an area than a residential street or an industrial district because changes are easily seen, and people gather there.

In examining commercial areas, I will start at the level of individual stores and establishments, then move up in scale to the street, though occasionally going back to the smaller units. Finally, I will discuss types of commercial areas.

Individual Units

There is no problem finding things to look at in a store or other commercial establishment; that is exactly what one is supposed to do. Some helpful indicators are: the *type* of establishment (what it sells or the service it provides); the quality of what is offered; physical size, layout, and method of display (including fixtures); the age of the place; the inventory and its completeness; the level of maintenance; the types and numbers of workers and clients; and details such as signs and *safety devices.* All are important; all exist in relation to one another, and together they can tell us something about the area in which they exist.

The possible combinations of clues and meanings are endless, but the messages are fairly straightforward. Consider some examples. People generally like to buy groceries at a store convenient to their home, so grocery stores usually mean a residential area nearby. A large grocery store needs a larger population to support it. If a good-sized grocery store has no nearby parking space for cars, it must be serving a high-density residential or working neighborhood; otherwise the store won't stay in business for long.

A store's goods or services tell something about the people served, no matter whether they live nearby or come from a larger area. High-priced goods indicate a high-income clientele. An ethnic bookstore suggests either a large, dispersed ethnic population or a nearby area where that ethnic group is or was dominant. Laundromats serve people in the neighborhood.

The presence of a number of older, apparently successful stores suggests stability. A store's age can be determined by the types of fixtures, specific signs ("Established 1960"), and inventories. The display and interior design can suggest how long the business has been there and whether it strives to stay up to date. New shops indicate change and a feeling of confidence, at least in the proprietors. A thin but varied inventory

may suggest a new business starting on a shoestring or a proprietor who is unsure of the market. A shopkeeper sitting alone in a store with an old and limited inventory may be paying very little rent or may own the building. One guesses that there is not a high demand for space in the area. One can tell whether a store is busy or not. A sign may be handmade or professionally made. It may tell that the store is one of a chain. A name can convey stability (Bank of America) or the origin of the building (Meat Market Coffee House). Even the lack of a sign is a clue. Guards at the door or grilles over the doors and windows at night signal a concern for security. Goods displayed on the street suggest the opposite. In each case the implication is fairly clear.

One type of commercial establishment that is particularly telling is a real estate office. The pictures in the windows tell what houses and stores are for sale, with prices. They sometimes display historic maps and photographs of the area. Then, too, one can ponder the meanings of the business itself—whether it has been around for a while (they like to say so, suggesting stability), or seems new or is about to go out of business.

The sizes of stores, the nature of goods or services sold, and the prices, combined with other characteristics of the surrounding area, suggest whether the shoppers are local or not. Usually, the larger the store, the more people are needed to support it, and therefore the less likely it is to serve the neighborhood primarily. The more specialized the goods or service (a Rolls Royce showroom, for example) and the higher the prices, then the wider the area served. A single store selling expensive, high-fashion dresses may serve a local market if it is one of a kind in a small commercial area. In all of these cases, the larger context is more useful in gaining an understanding of the dynamics of the area.

Commercial Streets

Stores and services are not usually alone in an area. In older communities stores are usually clustered on one or more commercial streets. At the street scale one looks for variety in types of stores or services, local or broader orientation, size of store, and the orientation of entrances; the condition and maintenance of the street, the number of people, availability of parking, access, and the nature of public improvements. It is at the street scale that change is most easily seen.

The variety of stores simply indicates the kinds of the people and activities being served and to some extent whether it is a local or nonlocal market. Local, of course, can mean whatever the observer decides: the immediately surrounding neighborhood as opposed to the city, or the city as opposed to the metropolitan area, and so on. By local, I mean the immediately surrounding area. The local or nonlocal orientation of a shopping area is not always clear. Some shops may serve people from both near and far. Nonetheless, the mix of stores and the dominance of one type is usually observable.

If the stores and services of a commercial street serve the local area, their nature can be a clue to the kinds of people living nearby. Stores with ethnic names and signs in different languages obviously suggest the ethnicity of the surrounding population. If all of the stores sell the same quality of merchandise, then the population is probably quite homogeneous in income. Price-level variation among the same types of stores, say inexpensive and high-priced groceries, suggest a mix of residents, particularly if both types have been there for a while.

One usually has a sense of the area's quality of maintenance, though it is sometimes difficult to pinpoint. In Copenhagen the quality and type of goods sold at one end of the Strøget (the main shopping street) is different from that at the other end, and the quality of store and building maintenance is also different. Generally, the physical quality of the stores differs from one shopping street to another. The differences suggest something about the economic status of the areas and, by extension, of the people they serve.

The number of people and the amount of car and bus traffic indicate how busy the shopping area is and perhaps also how well it is doing; the more people, the better business is.

A city-owned, public, off-street parking lot in an older shopping area may have been created to meet changing shopping habits—and perhaps a decrease in transit ridership—and to remain competitive with newer shopping centers. Its presence may also reflect the political strength of a local merchants' association, which was able to convince the city to develop the lot.

Areawide street improvements, such as planters, banners, coordinated sign designs, and ornamental lighting may represent action by a merchants' group or by the city. In any case, they represent special efforts to improve or maintain business, perhaps in response to a perceived decline.

Indications of change, often readily apparent, give information about the surrounding area as well as about the commercial area itself. New stores in a context of older ones might indicate neighborhood pressure to upgrade and possibly a new population group (younger, higher-income) moving in. A few older, marginal stores among many new ones might mean some favorable leases still in effect, but perhaps not for long. The message of recent vacancies is clear: business has left and, depending on how many have left and how recently, the implications for those remaining may be ominous. Changes from one type of tenant to another, upward or downward on the economic scale, tell of the markets for space and for shoppers. Public offices or social institutions occupying former storefronts usually mean the shopping area is declining.

Clues about expansion are often found at the edges of commercial areas. New stores or off-street parking along the side streets of a commercial area and in the adjacent residential area are a sign of expanding commercial use and perhaps also a signal that the housing may be vulnerable to change. On a side street a house immediately adjacent to a shopping street is often a less desirable residence than one farther up the street. The condition of such houses may suggest their relative desirability, and the demand for housing. The architectural attention to the edges of commercial areas and to parking lots can suggest how much the merchants care

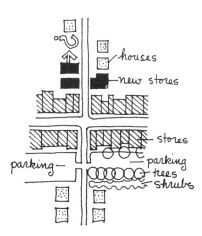

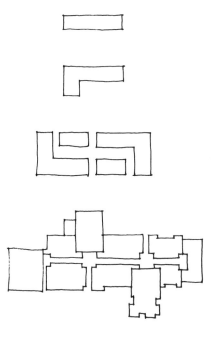

about their relationship to abutting property owners, as well as the relative political strengths of the two interests.

Commercial Centers

Any number of common terms are used to refer to types of commercial centers: neighborhood or regional center, mall, strip, enclosed mall. The different terms usually have more to do with the size of the market served than with anything else. A convenience center is usually small and provides a limited selection of goods and services — a grocery store, laundromat, and bank, say — to the immediate neighborhood. A regional center serves a wider market.

Most commercial centers are conceived and developed as a unit, usually with a parking area that serves all the stores. Design elements — building materials, signs, colors, trim details — are much more uniform than on commercial streets, a uniformity enforced by centralized ownership and management. The control may extend to the hours that stores are open, and the design of individual stores and window displays.[13] Indeed, if one sees such a center where design and maintenance uniformity are no longer in effect, it may be a clue that the central management has not been able to enforce its standards, a result of less than optimum financial clout. It is afraid of losing tenants.

Highway Strips

A strip — commercial development with off-street parking in front or rear along a wide, fast-moving traffic artery — usually stands alone, a divider between residential areas on either side: it is an edge, not a center. Strips have been characterized as transitional areas, where a business can set up easily, sell goods easily, often to people on the move, and, if necessary, move out quickly.[14] That characterization may be extreme, but the types of stores on a strip, their ages, and quality will reveal as much. If the area is dominantly utilitarian (auto sales, gas stations), if the people on either side of the strip are unlikely to know each other, and if few residents value the businesses, it may be a sign that it is easy to effect public or private change in the area. A street widening, for example, would be more easily achieved.

A commercial establishment standing alone raises questions. Why is it there? A single furniture store on a street amid buildings of a totally different nature may be there because an entrepreneur believes the location will be good for business. Or it could mean something more. Depending on the age and type of building, such a use can signify an older, now abandoned transportation route (the marginal motel on a bypassed main street). Or the builder may have anticipated that the area would develop rapidly, but it never did. The use that stands alone makes us ask why. The answers, even tentative ones, help us create hypotheses about the history and evolution of the area.

Downtowns

Downtowns are a special category, but the same indicators apply. We expect a central business area to serve a larger than local population, and we look for clues to the nature and economic stability of a wider area.

Some uses that one often finds in downtown areas are corporate offices, large older department stores, hotels, perhaps the best jewelry store in town, and certain government offices, such as the court or city hall.[15] The existence of these uses, the amount of activity associated with them, and the condition of the buildings tell something of the importance and the economy of downtown in the larger area. Other key indicators are the size of the downtown area; the variety of uses; building types, designs, condition, and age; the level of maintenance of public areas; the amount of new construction or renovation of old buildings; the number of people using the downtown, particularly the shopping area; and the nature and use of the transportation system.

Downtown edges can be particularly telling for signs of change: new construction or renovation pushing outward from the area, or vacancies and marginal uses suggesting contraction. The height of existing buildings may also delineate an edge, often one at which there are pressures for change.

Because a downtown is a center by definition, we expect traffic to be concentrated there, particularly public transit. So we look to see whether there is public transit, and if so, what kind. Studies have been done of the kinds of office-commercial concentrations and of the location and density of residential areas that are likely to be able to support public transit.[16] The kinds of transit—buses, subways, both, or neither—and the presence or absence of posted schedules and routes tell us how important downtown is as well something about the outlying residential areas. If there is a subway station for outbound trains, many people must live in the outlying area who come downtown to shop or work. If the only public transit is buses on limited schedules, we can guess that the residential area is low-density and dispersed and that the downtown is not very concentrated.

The type of transit may indicate a community's feelings about what the downtown should be (strong, city-centered) as well as what the outlying areas are like (compact, land-conserving). Many cities, including Calgary, Toronto, San Francisco, and San Diego, have built rapid transit systems, at least in part to achieve those kinds of development patterns. Increasingly, the health of public transit is an indicator of public will rather than of private market forces.

Street widths, amount of auto traffic, and provision of off-street parking go with transit as indicators; more auto-oriented facilities may mean less public transit. Large areas of ground-level off-street parking, particularly with wide or widened streets and older buildings, usually mean a change from an earlier, more intense downtown, now supplanted by outlying shopping centers and office parks. The off-street parking where buildings once stood may be an interim use, waiting to be developed.

The Public Environment

As much as 30 percent of the developed land in urban areas is used for public streets and walks. That public space is full of indicators of historical development, changes, values, and issues.

Street Names

Communities name and number their streets so that people can locate each other with relative ease. Numbered streets indicate the distance from some starting point, usually a center. Numbered streets can tell of unfulfilled expectations too, like a 243rd Street that exists only as a name or that has a wilderness between it and a real 71st Street. Front Street is likely to be along a waterfront or a former waterfront that has been filled; Main Street was intended to be just that; Bay Street once ran along the bay or led to it. (But be cautious about reading too much into Grandview Avenue or Shiplane Mews in the suburbs, or even Riverside Boulevard if the river is not there.) Street names may tell of local events and heroes; in Rome the street signs have captions to explain what the person did to be so honored.

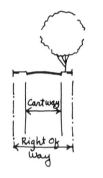

Street Widths

Street rights of way and their cartways (the distance between curbs, where curbs exist), are of different widths. Generally, older streets are narrower than newer ones. Generally, too, the width of the right of way reflects the relative value of the land when it was laid out, as well as reflecting community standards then and the anticipated importance of the street. The street may have been built wide enough to accommodate fire engines, permit a horse and carriage to turn around, or to permit two lanes of traffic with curb parking. When streets are wide and there is little traffic, it is worth asking why. What was the expectation for this street? Was the width a standard, a reflection of history, a sense of values?

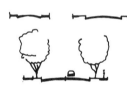

Obviously, an unpaved street indicates little wheeled traffic, and generally the higher the quality of the paving, the more likelihood of heavy use. The use of curbs to separate the roadway from the rest of the right of way is usually another sign of the community's desire to accommodate traffic. The designs of the roadway can also indicate a desire for a special character, as shown by wide, planted median strips, or designs

associated with country lanes, with neither curbs nor walks. Street design may also reflect an analysis of and concern for a special problem, such as slowing traffic or keeping through traffic away from local streets.[17]

Changes in street layouts are usually observable, even after considerable time has passed: one stretch of right of way is wider than the rest, sidewalks are suddenly narrower, trees are new or have been cut down, the paving becomes narrower, a crack in the street indicates where curbs once were, a traffic barrier exists that is not common to other streets. Those changes tell of solutions to problems and the values prevailing at the time the changes were made. One can recognize present or upcoming problems, for example, in heavy traffic on a two-lane residential street or in a temporary traffic diverter that shows signs of abuse.

Sidewalks

In some communities the streets are lined with houses on fifty-foot lots, but there are no sidewalks. That may have been a decision by the designer of the area, the housing developer, or the community to achieve some preconceived image of a desired environment. Or the neighborhood may have wanted sidewalks but did not have enough clout to get them. In some suburban areas sidewalks start and stop abruptly, for no apparent reason and without relation to the age of development. That can be because of area annexation patterns and timing: the streets without walks were developed before those areas were annexed to the city, when there were no sidewalk requirements. Sidewalks are usually built to community standards. A close look at them can sometimes reveal when the area was developed, or when improvements were made, or an earlier public works program, such as those of the 1930s that left dates in the walks. Contractors used nameplates to stamp their name and often the date in their work, but this is done less often now. In the 1970s and 1980s, new sidewalks and paving in an older area, particularly if accompanied by extensive property rehabilitation, is one indication of a publicly sponsored improvement program.

Sidewalk materials can also be telling. Concrete and asphalt are the most common materials in the United States. The use of brick or tile or an unusual design reflects an attempt to gain attention or to denote public pride.

Curbs

Curbs are used to delineate the uses within the public right of way and to channel water for drainage. The absence of curbs may mean that those functions are not required or that the community wants to maintain a less urban character. In American cities the age of curbing is usually apparent in the color and freshness and in signs of aging, such as cracks and settling. Granite used to be the standard curbing material, but these days less expensive materials, such as concrete, sometimes with a metal edge, or asphalt, are used. Granite curbing is used only for high-status projects. New curbs may have been installed because of a public improvement program, perhaps for new utility lines.

Street Trees

The story persists that San Francisco had very few street trees until Russian Premier Khrushchev visited and commented on that fact. Then, the story goes, the city started a tree planting program. In some city areas residents have displayed an active dislike of and resistance to the planting of street trees because they are messy, drop sap on cars, and require care. But a lack of street trees does not necessarily mean that the residents dislike them. Among the many possible explanations, such as disease, is the simple one that nobody thought of them.

If the trees on a street are all of one type and size, they were probably planted when the street was first developed. If they look younger than the houses, they may have been planted as part of a public project at a later time. If the trees are of different ages and species, people may have planted them individually over time. If they are all the same age but different types, then maybe the initial idea was collective but there were differences of opinion about the most appropriate type.

Or, one person could have started planting and the idea then spread. The trees themselves may grow at different rates and may look old or young depending on climate and care variables.

Street trees often fall victim to street widening. That may be obvious if the trees were removed only on one side or not continuously. We can tell how much the residents value trees when a street has been widened and the trees kept, even in the middle of the street, as is often the case in European cities.

Maintenance

The maintenance of public ways is usually a public job, though residents and merchants are often responsible for keeping sidewalks maintained. In most societies there is some expectation that the public ways should be clean and in good condition. When that expectation is not met, or if it is obviously surpassed, then questions form in the observer's mind. Is the refuse on the street a consequence of the time of day or week? Are all the streets in San Jose this clean, or only the ones in Naglee Park? Is there a direct relationship between the condition of the streets and the size and quality of the homes? If so, what does that say about who has influence? Is there a relationship between the number of potholes and amount of refuse and the city's financial situation?

Pavement cracks can tell another story, particularly if they are continuous and fairly straight. Such cracks tend to return in spite of repairs, because the foundations of the street on one side of the crack are different from those on the other side, representing different periods of construction. Settling takes place unevenly, causing the cracks. Being aware of them, one can tell of earlier changes, particularly street widenings.

Street Patterns and Layouts

If you go to a part of a city where the streets are narrow, close together, and irregular, you are probably in the oldest section. Try an area where the streets curve gently but regularly, and there is a good chance that it was developed after the turn of the century. A less

formal street pattern, with intersections farther apart, and more cul de sac streets, is further from the center and was developed more recently. Once set, street patterns tend to persist or to at least leave reminders of their presence. Street patterns and lot layouts provide clues to the area's history, the pace of development, major events, and public projects. Useful distinctions in looking at street patterns are regularity, scale and size of blocks, and breaks, seams, or cuts in a pattern.

Regular and Irregular Patterns

Streets in a regular pattern were laid out deliberately by a developer or the community. It is helpful to know the types of layouts associated with different times and places as well as the subtleties within eras. Most early European cities, for example, had walls, and the major roads usually fanned out from the city gates in radial patterns. In older American towns, radial road patterns are common. Such a road is probably from the nineteenth century or earlier, and the development along it has had an extensive history. Irregular street patterns imply that the area has developed incrementally, without conscious plan, in response to various forces and events.

A regular street system overlying or cutting through other patterns is usually the result of a major public project, perhaps an attempt to bring order to a less orderly system, almost always to improve transportation. The Paris boulevards of the 1800s may be the best known of many examples. Deviations within an otherwise regular pattern invite one to look for reasons: an institution or building that was important enough to cause the street to be rerouted; an obstructing topographic feature to be accommodated; a recent development that either closed streets or caused them to be rerouted. Alternatively, areas of irregular road patterns within a larger, more regular pattern may indicate older settlements, perhaps independent communities at one time, that have become part of a growing metropolis. Up until the late 1960s in the United States, irregular street patterns, especially with small blocks and many small buildings, were thought to be inefficient and

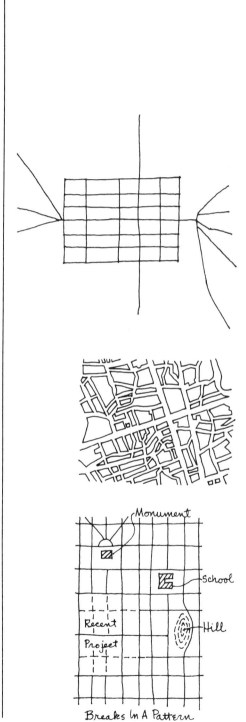

Breaks In A Pattern

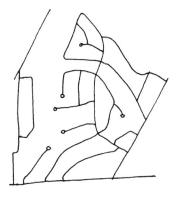

associated with slum conditions. Such patterns were considered reason enough for public acquisition and demolition of the area.

The curvilinear street patterns commonly found in suburban developments built after World War II were first used in the late 1800s. To be sure of the period when an area was developed, one must look for other clues, such as the age and style of buildings, location in the region, and street widths. Alternatively, an irregular and curved street pattern may have been topographically determined.

Scale and Size of Blocks

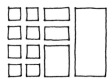

Areas of small blocks are usually older than areas of large blocks, except in large industrial areas or where a special use occupied a large land holding at an early time. Large blocks, now believed to be a more efficient use of land, have been a part of land assembly practices by large public and private developers. They are believed to provide a scale and pace consistent with the automobile, because fewer intersections permit greater speed, and with fewer streets, they are less costly to build and maintain.

Larger blocks within a smaller block pattern then may suggest recent development in an older framework. A public role in the development is a strong possibility because the city would have had to relinquish older streets to achieve the new pattern. Also the city government may have used its powers of eminent domain to assemble the land.

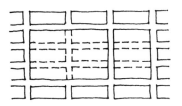

Breaks, Seams, and Cut-Throughs

Few cities have only a single street pattern; most have at least two main patterns and many variations. The breaks, or seams, where two patterns come together, or where a boulevard or freeway cuts through an otherwise continuous street pattern, are worth studying.

Usually, areas with different patterns were developed at different times. The place where two patterns come together can be where two separate communities or developments merged, but more often the break or seam represents a change in community policy resulting

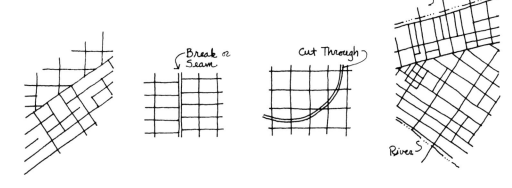

from a change in physical orientation (say from one river to another), a change in design style (rectangular to curvilinear) or a change in standards (small to large blocks). A cut through a pattern may have been there in the first place—a stream, a railroad line—and ignored in the initial street layout.

The places where two or more street patterns come together often are centers of activity, places of exchange, focal points. Times Square in New York comes immediately to mind. One's view is stopped by buildings along such seams, calling attention to the break. Buildings have to be accommodated to odd-shaped parcels, and the resulting differences are likely to be eye-catching. The purpose of a boulevard that cuts through an underlying pattern may have been to focus new development on the boulevard or its end points.

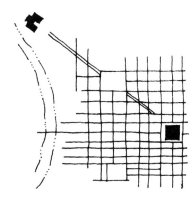

Breaks that separate areas of different activities often feel like no man's lands, areas of transition or division. Market Street in downtown San Francisco has for years been a dividing line between more and less desirable sections, a barrier that is being overcome only by an extraordinarily strong demand for offices, plus major public construction and changes in zoning policies. There is often a transition area between the downtown and areas developed later, as in Pittsburgh between the Golden Triangle and the Hill, in San Francisco between downtown and the Mission District, and in many cities where rail lines create divisions.

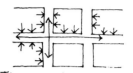

The larger South of Market blocks are more amenable to larger buildings and have a stronger orientation to the main streets which do not lead to Market St.

Not only is Market Street wider than the others, the block sizes on either side are significantly different. North of Market the small, squarish blocks have a neutral orientation.

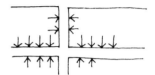

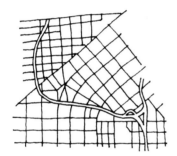

No man's lands, which by definition are the least well known, are vulnerable to change, particularly to major public developments, such as a freeway or other transportation line. If a change of that nature has already taken place, a look under or around it will tell whether the area is still a no man's land. New construction in out-of-the-way areas may reflect strong pressure for development. Where land is plentiful and demand light, no one will invest in the areas along seams. In most cases it takes a major private or public effort to overcome the poor image of a no man's land.

Building Arrangement

This term refers to the physical relationship of buildings to each other and to the street, the approaches and entry paths to buildings, and the ways in which buildings delineate spaces. To a considerable extent these matters concern the transition from public to semipublic and private areas. Building arrangement can be an indicator of community values and concerns as translated first into government regulations and then into physical realities. It can also be one indicator of the likelihood or extent of neighboring and community cohesiveness and organization. In considering building arrangement as an indicator of values or of the extent of communication among people, it is necessary to step gingerly. So many variables affect both values and communication.[18]

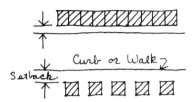

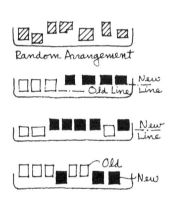

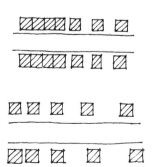

Buildings usually line up along a street; that is, they are set back a uniform distance from the pavement or sidewalk. Generally, the setback is greater on newer streets, at least in the United States, though there are important exceptions. Setback distance can reflect common practice or can be mandated by city regulation. Communities have been concerned with setbacks from the street at least since medieval times, sometimes for reasons of health (light, air, quiet) but often for purely aesthetic reasons. Health may have been the initial reason for setback regulations in the United States, but in recent years functional concerns, such as the possibility that the street will have to be widened—combined with cultural and design concerns have been the determining factors. In America a deeper setback is usually associated with a higher standard of living. Also, once a minimum setback line has been established, few buildings are placed further back. Because of these conditions, one can expect the following. A random building arrangement reflects a lack of regulation and probably a number of builder-developers; greater uniform setbacks are more recent than lesser setbacks; one or two buildings set closer to the street than the others in a line probably were built earlier; if they are new, however, they reflect either a recently changed regulation (attended by community concern) or the breaking of an unregulated norm (the community may then regulate to keep others from doing the same).

Breaks from the established pattern of back or side yard building setbacks also indicate that this problem has been a community issue. We tend to think of larger yards as "better."

I hypothesize that the farther removed from the street a building is either by distance or other barrier, the less likely that the residents or business are closely associated with the street and with day-to-day public life. In other words, the orientation of a house removed from the street is inward and self-contained. The closer buildings are to each other, the more likelihood there is of eye contact between their occupants. People who see each other often, I think, know more about each other. Clearly, then, the location of entries, windows, and walkways increases or decreases the possibilities of contact between neighbors. I hypothesize that building arrangement can determine the likelihood of people in them knowing each other (or the ease of getting to know each other).

Further, people living in close contact are more likely to form community associations and to respond to issues that may be of concern to all. Intervening variables, especially people's individual interests and needs, may be so important as to make building arrangement inconsequential. But if one observes several indicators, for example, deep setbacks, heavy traffic on the street, and entryways that do not encourage visual contact, then one could confidently predict that the neighbors know little about each other.

On a stretch of 24th Street in San Francisco, one observes that the houses are not arranged in a way that allows neighbors to see and talk to each other. It is hard to pinpoint why, but it may be because the doorways are isolated and the sidewalks narrower than on other blocks (rear yard arrangements, however, might facilitate meetings). Also the traffic is faster here than on the intersecting streets, and the houses are on the short ends of blocks, so there are fewer per block. The intersecting streets have many more trees, which make them seem narrower than 24th. It seems likely that people living on this stretch of 24th do not know each other and that community participation in local issues is not strong.

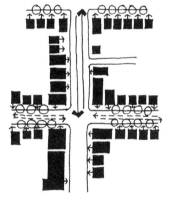

Topography

Those who live at higher elevations in a city usually have higher incomes than residents at lower elevations. Field experience in the 1980s suggests that Hans Blumenfeld's 1948 study of this phenomenon remains valid. There has not been any more recent work to confirm this.[19] The usual explanations for the correlation of elevation and income are that high locations are the most strategic and safe, are more costly to develop, and have the best views, most varied topography, and perhaps the best climate. However, the many exceptions to the rule demand explanations. Why might

lower-income people be living on the hills in one city? An undesirable neighbor, such as a factory that gives off smoke or noise may have made the higher elevation undesirable for higher-income people but not for those who work close by. The hill may have been relatively inaccessible in the past, and if the wealthier residents found more easily developed sites, the poorer residents may have been able to afford to build at the higher location. Blind land subdivision, done in a law office without benefit of (or care for) topographic data, with streets that could not be built on the hills, may have kept the land inaccessible and off the general market. In San Francisco the Bernal Heights, Potrero Hill, and Diamond Heights areas and in Pittsburgh the lower and upper Hill districts can be explained this way. Alternatively, a lower-income development at a higher elevation may have been built through public action, either at a time when the location was considered undesirable, or, as in the case of Diamond Heights, as a conscious effort to build an economically integrated community. Lower-income developments at locations that are otherwise desirable for topographic and other reasons are vulnerable to development pressures. In Rio de Janeiro some of the favelas may be cases in point, because the land is now more desirable, and on Telegraph Hill in San Francisco, higher-income people have moved in and taken over a formerly middle-income area.

Other natural factors that help one understand urban areas include sunlight (generally preferable to shade in temperate climates and avoided in others), noxious odors (to be avoided), and pleasant breezes. Geologic and soil characteristics suggest why some areas have not been built up. A river or other water source may have been the reason for the city's existence in the first place, and its major activities may be on the riverbanks. All these factors can be critical to the understanding we seek.

Location within the Urban Area

Sometimes it is easy to sense where one is in relation to a large urban area: walking along a route that leads from town, just outside of the downtown area or at the fringe of an urban area. Location is important, for it gives us some idea of what to expect. Generally in the United States population densities decrease as one goes away from the center of the metropolitan area.[20] If this is not the case, one should look for explanations, such as a smaller, once independent center that has been surrounded by outward development from the central city or from a nearby employment center. The higher-density area may be simply a small concentration of housing within a larger open area, masking an overall low-density pattern. In American cities poor people are more likely to live near the center, and middle- and upper-income people farther out; in most European and South American countries the pattern is the opposite. Again, knowing and expecting those patterns to prevail helps us understand when they do prevail and alerts us to look for special circumstance when they do not.

Location involves more specific expectations. Many railroad stations and yards, which were built near the centers of American cities, have fallen into disuse since World War II. If the demand for development is strong, the stations and yards are prime sites for alternative uses. Because of the large amount of land, a new development will have a major impact on the surrounding area. Many entrepreneurs will be interested.

Other activities have changed their locations — the wholesale food markets have moved to the outskirts of cities along with other truck distribution centers — and still others can be expected to generate demands in the future, such as tourist and convention centers. Communities whose location and development are dependent upon cheap transportation and energy costs are likely to feel pressures for changes in services and lifestyles if those costs rise sufficiently. Those communities could become less desirable. Location, then, is not only an indicator of what is normal in an urban area; it can also suggest issues that will arise in the future.

Conclusions

One could extend this list of observable physical indicators almost indefinitely. I have tried to discuss the clues that are most often used to raise the questions we need to answer.

If I were to add a tool at this point, it would be *maps,* which make the connection between "reality" and abstraction, including all the information that comes with nonvisual analytic methods. I always have a map in my mind, but there is nothing quite like the kind you can hold in your hand — whether it's a street map purchased at a gas station or a detailed map showing buildings and topography — to confirm street patterns, breaks, edges, locations, transportation routes, relationships among areas, and much more.

Many of the clues I have mentioned relate to economic status or economic forces. A general conclusion is that people's economic status is likely to be observable in their physical surroundings. Peirce F. Lewis's axiom that nearly all items in the human landscape reflect culture certainly applies to the economic culture.[21] In urban areas those who are less well off in income or wealth occupy the less "good" physical situations in terms of size, condition, maintenance, and location. It is important, however, to know something of the geographic (cultural-locational) context to make the most meaningful interpretations of the clues.[22] The less good the physical surroundings, in terms of the community standard or norm, the poorer the people who live in, work in, and frequent the area. The opposite — better surroundings, greater wealth — seems also true.

If we stopped to listen to our daily conversations, we might be surprised at how often we use words like *nice, large, small, good,* and *bad.* First observations in an urban area often use phrases like: "These are large houses" or "There is a lot of traffic and noise here" or "These buildings are in bad condition." The imprecisions of these words may be a result of observing many things simultaneously; they are short-cut conclusions. Regardless, all of the words reflect a value or bias of the observer.

To the extent that big–small, good–bad adjectives reflect personal standards — and may therefore mean something entirely different to another observer — it is particularly important to ask what the descriptions mean. What do I mean by "in poor condition" or "small units"? Many of the words have to do with sizes and amounts — widths of buildings or streets, amounts of traffic and people, costs of houses or cars. Other words refer to frequency — how often do we see "For Sale" signs, how often do we see that type of store. Many frequencies are quickly measurable in the field, and by measuring the sizes of buildings or land parcels or the widths of streets, by counting cars and people and doorbells, we define what we mean by "big." We can compare what we find not only with our personal knowledge but with other norms and standards as well. In short, we must try to step outside our personal standards or biases by being aware of the terms we use, by measuring, counting, and specifying, and by comparing observations. To be sure, our values prevent us from seeing some elements, let alone measuring them. There is no getting around that problem, but we can work to be more aware of what we are doing.

What one sees can be compared to a codified community standard. As I have noted, all nations, states, and communities have standards for what is built, usually aimed at upholding the health and welfare of the community. In one sense the standards represent the values, even biases, of the community. They usually take the form of laws or regulations concerning such matters as structural elements, light and air in rooms, room sizes, number of people per room, lane widths of streets. If we know something of those standards, we can compare them to what is seen, we can say consciously that what we are seeing is above, below, or the same as a known standard. In the Chinatown area of San Francisco, we may see an upper-floor living unit that is 10 by 12 feet.[23] We know that units this small would not be allowed today, so we can rightly call them small. It is then reasonable to take the next step and hypothesize that by the standards of the community there is a crowding problem, and that the community may decide to do something about it.

Many building standards, especially those for space, go well beyond demonstrable requirements of health and safety. In some ways, by comparing our vague adjectives with codified standards we are trading our own biases for those of the community.[24] Nonetheless, having started to question what we see and the descriptive terms we use, we should continue that questioning in field observation, particularly if the standards are likely to be the basis for some future action for change. It makes some sense to ask if what we see, regardless of its size or quality, is dangerous or inimicable to life. Usually it is not.

Modifying words such as *likely, suggests, probably,* and *might* appear over and over in discussing the clues and their meanings. Those words reflect the reality of this kind of analysis. We are not looking for data that can be manipulated and arranged so that all the parts add up to 100. We are looking for understanding.

If there are no studies that interpret what is seen, the clues are the only basis for hypotheses as to the meaning of what is observed. When one observes small houses, one guesses that they were built for modest- or low-income people. In the absence (unlikely) of any other clues to confirm or modify that hypothesis, one would assume that the present occupants are also low-income. Seeing a lot of refuse in a street generates a number of possible hypotheses, among them that the street cleaners have not yet worked there that day or that week; because of a financial crisis the city has curtailed this public service; the neighborhood has little influence in city hall; clean streets are not important to the people of this area or to the people of this city. Other clues, such as signs saying that the street will be cleaned on Friday (and we are seeing them on Thursday), or refuse-strewn streets all over the city, or dirty streets only in low-income areas, would help narrow the range of hypotheses and ultimately the conclusions. The relative cleanness of the street would be used in helping to deal with other subjects. It is easy to see that an indicator may have numerous meanings in combination with all the other clues. The message is clear: to be open to many possible meanings of specific indicators, except in those situations where the meanings are precise.

The lack of accumulated knowledge about cities seems to be one major difference between the kind of observation and diagnosis discussed here and that of other, more "scientific" pursuits. For example, much more is known of body chemistry, human physical structure, and biological systems than is known of urban chemistry, urban structure, and urban systems. I doubt if urban clues ever can be as precise or their meanings so well known as clues in other fields of inquiry.

This exercise of looking at clues and pondering their meanings is not strictly analogous to Hercule Poirot-type detective work, where the objective is to find how a particular antisocial act came to happen and who was responsible, using a much more limited set of clues. But there are important similarities. As in medical diagnosis and criminal detective work, in urban diagnosis the observer looks for patterns, breaks in the patterns, and deviations from the norms. Perceiving new or foreign elements in a field, one asks why and how and what are the meanings? The similarity to detective work may lie in openness to seeing relationships and in a questioning way of thinking. The clues are the critical starting point.

4 Observing and Interpreting East Walnut Hills

It is June 1981, a gray, warm, muggy morning, about 9:15, in Cincinnati. We are at the intersection of Madison Road and Torrence Parkway, about three miles northeast of downtown, having driven along the Columbia Parkway, which skirts the Ohio River. In driving here we did not see much of the city, since we went along the river, but we did see some rather nice-looking houses on the bluffs overlooking downtown on the east. This is known as the East Walnut Hills section of the city.

Most of the buildings we see were built in the period from before the turn of the century (simple brick or wooden structures that remind us of buildings in the East) to the 1920s or 1930s (more horizontal, rough brick, like a lot of buildings seen in one's childhood in Cleveland). The buildings are not more than three floors high, except for a new six- or eight-story brown brick apartment or condominium building.

At the northwest corner is an old building, recently converted to a bar and restaurant. The sign and some window frames are new, and the brick looks as if it has been recently sandblasted. It looks like the kind of place where young executives go for drinks after work or for lunch or dinner: stylish, lots of brick and old wood. The buildings on Madison Road come right to the sidewalk, with no front yards and few side yards. Stores and other uses that catch the eye: the Bible Deliverance Church, Second Unity Baptist Church, two antique stores, two small sporting goods stores, a music store, an art gallery near the western end of the building strip, but set apart. The stores are not open yet. The buildings and public areas are well maintained. The types of churches suggest a black population, but the

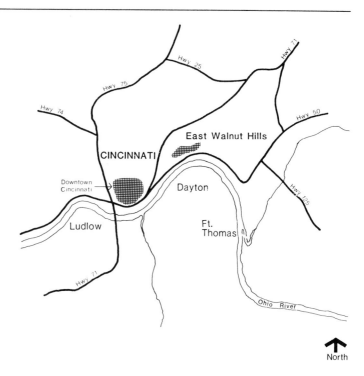

EAST WALNUT HILLS – CINCINNATI

Scale

stores hint of an area that has been black and is now changing to a white, professional, higher-income clientele. But it may not be a stylish area yet.

As we walk west on Madison we see very large, old, well-maintained houses and two old small parks near each other, Owl's Nest and Annwood, according to signs. The houses do not appear to have been subdivided (only one telephone line to each, few cars visible). The curbs are old stone but do not look like granite. The houses on one side street, Annwood Avenue, are also very large single-family homes, well maintained. But the maintenance of homes and yards is not of the highest quality, as would be shown by manicured lawns and shrubs, fresh paint every three to five years. Here some aging shows, some paint is needed. These large, older houses may have had live-in gardeners once, but not now. On one side street, Gregory, the

WALKING ROUTE IN EAST WALNUT HILLS – CINCINNATI

newer one- and two-story houses look expensive; the
lots are large, the setbacks deep, and the maintenance is
good. These houses are of the 1950s and 1960s.

The sidewalk contractor has left his mark on Madison
and on the first side streets: "W. R. Budd & Bro., Est.
1892, Cinti, Ohio." That does not mean the sidewalk
was laid in 1892, but the turn of the century would be
a good bet. We notice a police squad car, which is in
turn noticing the stranger-observers carrying cameras
and taking notes.

The Doherty School—Seven Hills Middle School is
well set back from the street with a very elegant painted
sign at the street—by these indications, a private
school. Do its students live in the immediate area, or do

they come from all over Cincinnati? Would a more exclusive school have a smaller sign or no sign?

On another side street, Fairfield, the homes are not nearly as large as those on Madison, but they are of roughly the same vintage: turn of the century and later. New asphalt roofing material is not as good as the old. Houses and yards are adequately maintained, not perfect. The owners seem to be fixing one problem at a time, setting priorities—maybe a new roof this year, fixing the porch next year, painting after that, a major landscape job sometime in the future. The houses were built as single-family homes and still are. A car bumper sticker says "NO NUKES." We see a lot of toys on two front porches. At the first corner a white man and woman, both in their thirties probably, are talking, then walk away. They are animated and appear purposeful—neighbors, not a couple. Further up the street a black man in his early fifties stands at his car talking to a white man in his late fifties. Two black boys, about ten years old, ride around on bicycles. Farther along Fairfield is a three-story apartment house, maybe built in the 1920s, middle class. Many houses have new, white street numbers on them, all the same kind.

In this area there is a sense of striving, of trying to improve. There is a sense, more than conclusive visual evidence, of a range of ages and a racial mix. We have seen some people talking, so it seems that neighbors know each other. We guess that they are actively trying to maintain this as an integrated area, racially and economically. Probably there is an active neighborhood association. It is not clear whether there is a public program for planning, rehabilitation, or code enforcement here, but it is a good bet that these people are in contact with city hall and that city hall knows them.

At a corner the man and woman we saw earlier are still talking. They say hello and ask what we are doing with camera and note pad. They say they are concerned that a stranger might be noting which houses have stained glass windows in order to steal them. When we explain our purpose, they say the neighborhood association of East Walnut Hills would be interested in our observations and conclusions.

On Cleinview Street, the houses and lots are smaller and more modest than on Fairfield. The street is not as well maintained, and the houses are closer to the street. Looking through windows we see that there are a number of vacancies. More of the people are black. Were these houses occupied originally by servants of wealthy people on Madison? From our starting point to Cleinview, the lots and houses have gradually gotten smaller.

When we turn back onto Madison, we see a church across the street on the south side. Later we note its name: Seventh Street Presbyterian Church. The stones are very clean, as if new. Something about the building looks strange, perhaps the roof.

Further along Madison is a new firehouse, built in 1979, according to a plaque. At the corner of Madison and Woodburn is a Catholic church, St. Francis de Sales, that has been around for a long time. Across the street a turn-of-the-century, multistory brick building, the San Marco Building, is being rehabilitated; the inside has been gutted, and new window frames and interior partitions have been installed. Also in this block is a boarded-up one-story structure with all the earmarks — marble facade, formal doorway, large spaced windows — of a bank. At a fourth corner an odd-shaped vacant lot has been graded, fenced, and sodded, and the grass has been trimmed recently. These are strong indications of a public program. The rehabilitation of the old brick building is probably being done through a public program rather than by a private developer. Is this a housing project with some local and federal input? Why is the vacant lot so nicely cared for and fenced, not overgrown and unkempt? It must have had buildings on it until recently. It seems as if a concentrated effort is being made to improve the area economically and to improve its image as well.

On Woodburn, as we walk southwest away from Madison, the buildings are built right to the sidewalks and there are no side yards. The Cruz Building has an 1895 date, and the others seem to be of the same vintage. The stores and people on the street tell us whom the area serves: hair salons with black customers

and stylists, second-hand stores, black teenagers, God's Holy Church. The block seems semivacant, with not much business. There are vacancies, not many people. This would be a hard area to plan for, because of economic and physical problems—low income, few jobs, few activities for kids, physical deterioration, vacancies. But if some buildings were cleared, residents would be displaced. At present there is probably no market to attract investment. If the city is actually involved in a program here then it might well be with a cautious, wait and see, look-for-opportunities-while-holding-on program.

Farther along Woodburn are two apartment buildings built in the 1920s or early 1930s; they are brick, two and three stories high, one in half-timber and stucco style. They were probably built for middle-income families.

The presence of the Cincinnati Suburban Bell Building suggests that this area was once considered to be suburban, even though it is only about three miles from downtown.

On a group of homes on one side street, aluminum siding has replaced the original siding material. The houses, small and reasonably well maintained, suggest working-class owners and renters. The people are mostly black. The homes on the next street, Locust, are somewhat larger and in better condition.

There are large parking lots, with many cars, on both sides of Woodburn at one point. From this vantage point we can see that Blue Cross occupies what used to be the Suburban Bell Building and that the parking lots are for the employees. Is Blue Cross here as part of a program to locate in poorer areas and employ local people? Many employees drive to work, but it is best not to draw any conclusions from this. The parking lots have fences and lockable gates and are very well lit, so it seems likely that car-directed crime is or has been a problem here and that there is a perception that it originates with local residents.

At the corner of Woodburn and East McMillan, still close to the Blue Cross complex, the area seems to be different. The Palette Studios and a furniture company are oriented to higher-income people. The employees are white. Across the street is St. Ursula Academy, a large building set back somewhat from the street. Except for St. Ursula, the area has a feeling of "hardness" whose source is difficult to define. There are times when one senses that one has entered a tense, no man's land; and it is very difficult to pinpoint why that feeling persists, but it is there. There is a feeling of transition here and of "resistance." Is there racial tension here?

A sign on the building next to St. Ursula's says "Herman Schneider Foundation." Who was Herman Schneider? Other signs indicate that a woman's club and an engineering society, in 1935, have used the building. A building that never quite found a use?

The next building on East McMillan is the New Thought Temple. The building looks more like a synagogue of the 1920s than like most churches. Perhaps it was founded by liberal Jews or ex-Jews. Is the word "Temple" an indicator of the earlier residents of this part of town? The evidence is too flimsy to say for sure. A black maintenance man says hello.

The small offices along this part of McMillan are not thriving. A building once occupied by Automatic Data Processing seems to have been adapted or modified many times. It is for sale.

The Walnut Hills Christian Church, built in 1924, is a solid stone structure that looks as if it serves an upper-middle-class congregation: it reminds us of a church in an English town, and we wonder if there was a conscious attempt to imitate that style.

Ingleside Avenue, off McMillan, has single-family, middle-class-sized homes. Most of the residents are black, probably the owners. At Madison and Woodburn the neighborhood was lower income, with some rental housing; along McMillan the housing is middle class and owner-occupied. The residents closer to Madison and Woodburn may always have been black, perhaps working as servants in the wealthier homes. One senses that the area is whiter close to McMillan.

As we walk east, the large homes on the south side

of McMillan bespeak early wealth, rather like the houses we saw earlier on Madison. The largest houses are on the south side of the street, where the view is of the river. A new high-rise condominium building is farther east on the south side of McMillan. The cars in the large parking lot are big; the people we see are older, mostly whites. This is market-rate housing that probably replaced an older mansion, indicating that the area is vulnerable to change. Past the condominiums is some new, low-rise housing. The older houses are oriented to the street, but the new housing, both the high-rise and the low-rise, is not. The high-rise, separated from the street by the parking lot, is probably situated to get a river view. The low-rise, too, tries to establish an independent environment.

The maintenance of houses improves as we walk east. Some houses on the north side of McMillan have two telephone lines and more than one doorbell, indicating that the houses have been converted to multi-family dwellings or that there are roomers. The walks go directly from the houses to the street over good-sized front lawns.

Traffic on McMillan, although not heavy, moves fast; the cars move through this area without stopping. This street is wider than the side streets and there are no cross streets in this section.

The people on the south side of the street seem to be a higher-income group than those on the north. Do the residents on each side know and talk to each other? Is there communication across the street? Probably not. As opposed to the feeling on Madison at the beginning of the walk, here it seems less likely that a strong neighborhood association exists. Without community involvement the neighborhood is more vulnerable to change, perhaps rapid change.

The housing on Cleinview, north of McMillan, is older and more modest. Some houses are not well maintained. A vacant building has a ''For Sale'' sign. There is trash in the yards, which are poorly kept up. Is it because of the difficult terrain? A simple white stone house has an 1850 date, much older than the others.

Good-sized housing, well removed from street; some converted to more than one unit?

←→ McMILLAN AVE. Rapidly paced traffic

Large homes, further removed from street, heavy landscaping

On the other side of the street, two older houses, but not as old as 1850, have been rehabilitated recently, and the work looks professional.

On Taft, which comes up from the river toward Woodburn and intersects with Cleinview, is a group of houses close together, built in the early or mid-1800s. At Taft and Moorman a brick house has been newly rehabilitated, another good job. Is this a small subarea that young people have "found"? A white woman is standing at Taft and Ingleside. The area south toward McMillan seems to be racially mixed, becoming more black west toward Woodburn and north toward Madison.

When we reach Madison, we again see the Seventh Street Presbyterian Church again. What is it about that church? The stone looks new or newly cleaned. The roof of the sanctuary has distinctly contemporary detailing, the sort of shopwork that is done today in joining metal with stone. But the steeple tower is old, as is a smaller one on the other side. If the sanctuary were as old as those towers, it would be larger. Aha! That's a *new* sanctuary. So what happened to the old one? Perhaps it burned and was rebuilt. The church could not afford to rebuild it to the original size, but the construction is very well done, expensive. If there was a fire, was it arson? Could it have been racially connected? All of this is very speculative, a long shot. It is interesting though, if all of these speculations are correct, that the church members chose to rebuild here rather than to leave the area.

Along Madison, as we walk east back to our starting point, we see that white children are leaving with their mothers and fathers. There is also a school there. They

walk to cars parked on Madison and on side streets to the north, so the school seems to draw students from some distance. Still more young students and parents are leaving the Doherty School grounds. The kids look well polished, upper class, with expensive hair styles.

The schools and churches have been here a long time. Although the people who originally lived in the area probably left slowly, the institutions that served them remain, serving the same kinds of people. The institutions could have moved, but perhaps the new market was not concentrated in one spot. Do the institutions feel committed to the area? We can't tell. If there is racial tension, it is not severe enough to push them out.

As we near the starting point, we wonder if some of the old single-family homes on Madison have been quietly converted to institutional uses that are not visibly announced. Maybe there *is* an announcement—there are more parked cars than you would expect for a single-family house.

At the small commercial area where this trip began, the gallery is open and two white men, stylishly dressed, are taking something out. We notice the Blue Wisp Jazz Club—a leftover from the recent time when this area was predominantly black?

Where do the residents shop for food, where did they shop in earlier days? The two major intersections, at Madison and Torrence and at Madison and Woodburn, would seem logical centers, but presently there do not seem to be any significant stores. The residents may have to drive to shopping centers out of the area. Is this an untapped market for new commercial development?

We again wonder how the very large houses on Madison can remain as single-family homes. The wealthiest people no longer live here, according to the lack of signs that the grounds are cared for by full-time help and the fact that the houses do not appear newly painted. In other cities, homes like this would have been converted to multi-unit rentals or institutional uses, or razed in favor of new apartment units. Are the present owners able to hire part-time maintenance help without too great a cost? Cincinnati may have a good supply of skilled property maintenance workers who work for fairly low wages. If that has been the case, will it remain so?

We conclude that the city has done some concentrated planning to stabilize this area, to upgrade the physical conditions or to build new housing. The fix-up work on houses on Fairfield, the new numbering shared by many houses, the housing rehabilitation work at Madison and Woodburn, the rehabilitation of older, maybe historic houses south of Madison are some indicators of this. The improvements seem to be scattered, as if those in charge of the program are feeling their way and having some trouble knowing what will work. They may be looking for individual opportunities for improvements, hoping that such an approach will be enough. If there is such a public effort, the residents are actively involved, at least in some areas.

Parts of the area were probably declining, but the decline has stopped for the most part, thanks to public and neighborhood attention. But about half of East Walnut Hills, the west and southwest, where the people are poorer, is vulnerable to economic, social, and physical decline; the least affluent people — and their neighborhood — are most vulnerable to economic cycles. The eastern part, on the other hand, seems to be in the process of modest gentrification. But some of the large expensive homes on Madison will in time be vulnerable to conversion or razing if the present or future owners are unable to keep on maintaining them. The residents should keep an eye on that possibility. The residents may not want to admit that there is pressure to convert, institutionalize, or raze and may be uninterested in possible solutions, except rigid enforcement of single-family zoning. If proposals to alter those houses do arise, it will be hard to discuss the matter and to develop alternatives in time. A city planner should be watching the area for signs of change and should have some possible solutions in mind.

Madison has a few characteristics of the English

High Street: the development faces a wide street, and here and there, usually at a major intersection, is a greater concentration of shops and houses. Was that the model along Madison? Were the intersection concentrations along Madison created by old roads from the river? Does the pattern continue beyond East Walnut Hills? These questions come to mind as the observation ends. It is 11:15 A.M. A light rain is beginning to fall.

Three knowledgeable staff members of the Department of Economic Development of Cincinnati and later two resident reviewers responded to our observations and diagnosis.[1] We were correct on most counts. More specifically, the observations about gentrification of the commercial area at Madison and Torrence are correct. The bar-restaurant, about a year old, was developed by a member of the City Council of Cincinnati. It is seeking a young executive clientele.

The residents shop at Hyde Park, a nearby shopping center that is very complete, a place where they have shopped for years. The Walnut Hills business district is nearby as well. Opinion is mixed, even among professional market analysts, as to whether there is a market for a new, locally oriented shopping center.

The large houses on Madison are single family, but two have been converted to institutional use. East Walnut Hills was once a very wealthy area, and some very wealthy people still live here, perhaps on side streets that we did not visit. The owners on Madison, fearful that the houses will be converted to apartments, are militant about keeping the zoning single family. That kind of conversion took place in an area to the east and is associated with downgrading and with racial tensions.

There is a commitment to retaining a racially and economically integrated neighborhood in the area immediately north of Madison. This has long been a mixed area of upper-income whites and lower-income blacks, and there is local pride in the fact and history of this integrated character. According to one reviewer,

more middle-income whites are now moving in. The
East Walnut Hills Assembly citizens' organization is active, especially in the Madison area.

The Seventh Street Presbyterian Church was fire-
bombed during Cincinnati's racial disturbances in the
late 1960s. The bombing may have been racially moti-
vated, but it has been suggested that someone associated with the church was responsible. The private
schools are expensive, and most of their students do
come from outside the immediate area.

There is a public program in the Walnut Hills area,
aimed at rehabilitation of housing and enforcement of
building codes. A Redevelopment Foundation—
something not perceived by the observers—is active in
this area. The San Marco Building being rehabilitated
at Madison and Woodward will provide subsidized
housing for the elderly. The sodded, fenced, and well-
maintained lot at this intersection is *not* publicly
owned, however. It was purchased by an insurance
company on the side of the block that we did not see
and is being held for future use.

Our perceptions about the Woodburn Avenue area
were correct. The director of the Redevelopment Foundation sees the area as hard to deal with. The foundation is taking a wait-and-see attitude while working
with existing owners to upgrade the area. Our conclusions about the active role of the City's Department of
Development in this area were largely correct, as were
our ideas of what racial and income groups live where.
A staff person who had lived in the area confirmed
that the people on the south side of McMillan do not
know each other for the most part; they are socially
and economically different from those on the north side.

A person whose parents live in the area and the
director of the Walnut Hills Redevelopment Foundation, responded in some detail to our observations and
prognosis about the large Madison Avenue homes.
Some of these houses are still occupied by very wealthy
people, but the others have been bought by couples
with combined incomes of from $40,000 to $200,000.
These people want to live in large, old houses even if
they cannot maintain them perfectly. They do much of

the maintenance themselves. The reviewers contend that area residents would strenuously resist proposals to permit conversion of these homes. Such a proposal was made in the late 1970s and was opposed. This is consistent with our field observations.

We also consulted available data and reports about East Walnut Hills to help check the readings and interpretations of the field observers. Most of the data is from the U.S. Census and from local studies. That kind of information does not usually cover or hint at the history of an area, levels of citizen activity, the nature of commercial areas, levels of current investment, social tensions, vulnerability to change, or other activity on a scale smaller than the census tract. The statistics tend to be out of date and do not convey the richness of detail and the dynamics we observed in East Walnut Hills. Observation does that! Secondary data can provide some long-term demographic and housing information for the area and the whole city.

The field investigation was silent about what was happening to the resident population of East Walnut Hills, though it might have been expected to provide some clues. Vacancies were observed, but only in passing. Between 1970 and 1980 the area population decreased by more than 24 percent, to 4,106, a significantly greater decrease than the whole city's 14.8 percent. It might be expected that such a drastic reduction in population would be more visible. However, the total number of housing units has stayed fairly constant since 1970, as has the number of households. The vacancy rate was 10.8 per cent in 1980. The number of persons per household has declined somewhat, a less visible characteristic than is other physical change.

Between 1970 and 1980 the black population remained fairly constant as a percentage of the total population (32–33 per cent), though the actual numbers dropped by 22 per cent. The field investigation observed where blacks and whites lived but did not discover changes in racial composition of the residents. We did guess that Madison and Woodward and the Cleinview area have probably been largely black for a long time and that one commercial area appears to be changing from a black-serving to a more affluent, white-serving area.

The overwhelming majority of housing units (93.5 percent) were judged to be in standard condition in 1974. The field investigation noticed only one small area of buildings in poor condition. Other census information neither confirmed nor refuted the diagnosis. A possible confirmation of the limited market for new housing in this area is the small number of permits for new construction between 1975 and 1982.

If available statistics do not give a sense of neighborhood dynamics, local residents make up for this lack. Neighborhood newspapers confirmed that East Walnut Hills in 1983 was an active area, with many people working to improve the physical, economic, and social environment.

All of the individual clues that I discussed in Chapter 3 were important in the field observation of East Walnut Hills. In practice, however, the clues combined with each other and with our knowledge almost unconsciously as we looked for answers to our questions: How is the area doing? What is it like to live here? Would I invest here, or would someone else? Are there problems? What is likely to happen in the future?

One ponders the answers, or possible remedies, to these questions, assuming the hypotheses are borne out by further study. Early on in our observation we wondered not only about the potential vulnerability of the large homes along Madison but also about possible solutions. Would it be appropriate to permit the building of additional structures on their large lots? How should that question be asked of residents who might not want to consider the problem? Should there be solutions ready? In another example, we wondered how to deal with the marginal uses and vacancies along Woodburn, and we considered the vulnerability to change of the big parcels along McMillan. But it is not one particular lot or one particular large house or vacant store that triggers the questions or the many possible answers. It is, rather, their relationships to each other and the larger context of the area.

5 Seeing Change

The physical, social, and economic fabric of cities
changes continually, in ways that are often interrelated.
When something new happens in a city, the residents
and their representatives, including city planners,
respond. People flock to meetings of the city council or
the planning commission to find out how the changes
will affect them or to report that they are being af-
fected. Residents may be alarmed about a new housing
development on vacant land because they did not
anticipate it or because the housing is different from
theirs. If a neighborhood has found that traffic has
gotten heavier, the residents will want something done
about the safety problems. When large old houses, like
those in Cincinnati, change to other uses, neighbors
became aware of it and want to know what it portends.
If a local shopping area or even a whole downtown
loses business over time, the merchants become wor-
ried, but they may not act in time to save the situation.

To be aware that change is happening, that it will
happen, or even that it is unlikely is the first step in responding to it, even if the response is to do nothing.
Quite often observation is a faster way to become
aware of change than are other research methods.

Changes between Areas

As a person walks or drives, he somehow knows when
he is passing into a different area. How does he know?
What was it that led walkers near a freeway, in the
Hayes Valley area of San Francisco, to conclude that
they were in an area of contention? Most often there is
a perception of change in the people, houses, arrangement of buildings or streets, street details, traffic, or
land uses—a change in the pattern of individual clues.

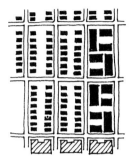

Most patterns are larger-scale versions of individual indicators: land uses that cover a whole area rather than a single site, many buildings of the same age, size, or arrangement, people with similar dress or physical characteristics, a uniform quality of materials and maintenance, or uniformity in public works such as walks, curbs, street widths, lights, and signs. Some characteristic of the area makes an impression, and the observer says, "This seems to be an area of "wealth," or of "poverty," or of "local shops." The observer does not necessarily start out with a specific checklist of patterns to be identified; such a checklist can hamper the process of observation. The identification of a new pattern that is not on any checklist may prove the most telling.

The lack of pattern, because of a mix of uses, sizes, or people, may be significant in comparing one area with another. In American cities, areas that are physically varied are also likely to be economically and socially diverse. The contrast between regularity and irregularity—street setbacks or land uses that are all the same and then become irregular, may be a signal of change from one area to another. Sometimes the clue is a progression from one quality or size or use or even population group to another.

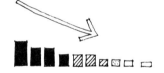

One sees geographic change in part by identifying patterns and being aware of where the patterns change or cease to exist, taking into consideration that patterns overlap. Good maintenance does not coincide with any particular type or size of building, for example.

Having identified a change between two areas, we begin to ask if the changes seem "normal." In a suburban community, for example, one would expect to observe a shopping center between areas of single-family detached homes; one would not expect to see a high-rise apartment building or an office development in the middle of the residential area. If the pattern or progression is not what one would expect—sharp delineations between developed and undeveloped land rather than the more normal urban sprawl into the countryside, say—one asks why and looks for explanations, perhaps a strong public policy against sprawl in this case. Another example would be a large tract of undeveloped land close to a city center. Maybe it is being withheld from development because of quirks of ownership or because of construction difficulties (a swamp) and will be built upon long after the outlying land is developed. Or a public program, such as urban redevelopment in the United States, which cleared large areas of many cities in recent decades, may explain the new pattern. The observer may not know enough about local history to be able to explain a pattern, and that recognition, too, is important.

Changes within an Area

Seeing change *within* an area may be different from identifying change between areas. It is more a matter of time than of scale. A change is taking place within a pattern, usually in the form of a "new" or relatively new element that is different, in substance or nature or just in its newness, from its surroundings. The features to look for are the *newness* of the clue within its context, its *nature* (such as size or quality) relative to the pattern, and its *amount.* Even if a new building is the same in design and detail as the older ones nearby, it differs because of its newness—in paint, wood, landscape, absence of weathering, or something else.

A new house that is significantly larger and made of more expensive materials than those around it, though of the same single-family type, suggests that the builder-owner either did not think about the difference in investment or concluded that the investment was safe, that the surroundings were either stable or would increase in value. If one sees a number of such houses, perhaps a new pattern, it may indicate a strong demand for expensive housing in the area. New housing with occupants along a street with heavy, fast traffic and mixed or nonresidential use, such as one finds on Valencia Street in San Francisco, suggests a strong demand for housing in the area and probably in the city as a whole. In such an environment a high vacancy rate or marginal uses would be more usual. One would not expect such investment in an environment that purchasers or renters "normally" would find less than

desirable. Nineteenth Avenue in San Francisco is another of those fast, high-volume, noisy streets where occupancy rates are high and new buildings can be seen.

New office structures may represent either abrupt change or continuation of an established pattern. In San Francisco's downtown one can see, in the relative ages of the various buildings, that office development has been continuous. In Calgary, Alberta, on the other hand, most of the new office buildings were built within the span of a few years. Look where the newest development is taking place and ask if there is a pattern to it, a direction of change. In San Francisco, the direction of new development is clearly into the area south of Market Street. But why is new office development not moving out in all directions from the old, *visible* core of Montgomery and California streets? Immediately to the west is Chinatown, small-scaled and old, and to the north the old, brick Barbary Coast area. Why hasn't the new development moved there? Have there been economic or culturally imposed constraints? It is important to deal not only with where development *is* going and why, but also with where it is *not* going.

On a smaller scale one can look for new stores — or no new stores — in an older shopping area: new signs, newly arranged and painted interiors, new fixtures, new stock. Having identified the newness, we then wonder in what other ways the store may have changed — type of goods? prices? style? Are the expected customers similar to or significantly different from those that use the older stores? Might such a change reflect a shift in the nearby population? If we saw a number of new stores within the older context, we would surely pursue the answers to these questions.

Rehabilitation can be a sign of newness. A concentration of new work on older buildings may be the result of nothing more than an astute and persuasive salesman of shingles or aluminum siding or windows. But the salesman was probably a good "reader" of the environment who understood that the buildings were ripe for rehabilitation and that the residents could be sold on his product. Or extensive new work in a neighborhood may signal some joint action, the result of a neighborhood campaign or a public program; this is especially likely if there are new sidewalks, curbs, and lighting. Or the new work might mean new owners with larger incomes than those they have displaced.

So the nature of the newness within existing patterns can tell something of the physical and economic direction of changes. If the "newness" is actually ten or fifteen years old within a still older pattern, we might wonder when and why the changes stopped. That, in turn, might lead to asking about the direction of future change.

How Much Change Is a Lot?

Two or three new houses on a street may not represent significant change. So how much change is significant? If one knows how often urban Americans move and approximately how many dwelling units there are in a block and makes allowances for the time of year when people are most likely to move, it is not too difficult to run through the arithmetic of how many "For Rent" or "For Sale" signs constitute "a lot." One can also compare the number and size of new or recent stores and offices on a street with the total of earlier buildings and uses to gain a sense of the proportion of new to older structures. Counting is the first step in answering how much is a lot of change, after which one might move to other research methods for verification.

Cycles of Change

Change is to be expected. The new and the different may be explained by the relationship of the area to some cycle. After twenty or thirty years, the owners of single-family residential homes built in the 1950s might be ready to move. Their families have grown up, or the housing requires major maintenance. So population shifts can be expected in the area. Ethnic areas, especially of immigrants, tend to change as their populations age and/or become assimilated. Industrial areas change, and buildings may become obsolete as technologies and products change. Warehouses are more adaptable to changes than buildings that house heavy industry. There appear to be cycles of office development and maturation as well. The cycles are not precise, and for older areas with mixed populations, the dynamics are muddy. Just being aware of such cycles can help explain the changes in an area.

Directions of Change

Walking along a street, one may start to observe a number of clues that are different from those that have been the pattern. Perhaps the people are different, or the building types and uses. The shift may not be abrupt. Is there a sense of geographical direction to the change? For example, in an area that is in the process of upgrading—expensive rehabilitation, more expensive stores, higher-income people—the clues that are new in the older pattern have their own pattern, one that suggests a geographical direction of change. It is like looking at a scatter diagram in which the elements form a pattern pointed in a particular direction or directions.

We go another step to ask: what factors can intervene to accelerate or to stop the direction and pace of observed change? A barrier can be physical, such as a wide, dividing street or a steep hill. Barriers within an area may be social, erected by residents or politicians who are determined to stop office expansion into a residential district, for example. External factors can intervene, such as a decrease in large-scale federal initiatives, as occurred with urban redevelopment. Or a change may stop because it is not consistent with economic forces in the area or the city. Triggered by observations, questioning should lead to further research that can help predict what is likely to happen.

Vulnerability

To be vulnerable is to be "capable of or susceptible to being wounded or hurt," "open to attack," or "difficult to defend." Sometimes physical clues can tell more quickly where an area is vulnerable to change than can demographic and economic statistics.

If one stands on the outskirts of an urban area with large-scale new construction on the right and farmland on the left, one reasonably concludes that the farmland

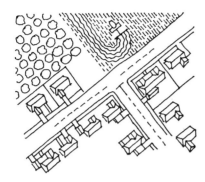

newly rehabilitated housing
"moving south" in 1970's
and 1980's ↓

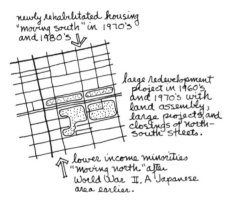

large redevelopment
project in 1960's
and 1970's with
land assembly,
large projects, and
closings of north-
south streets.

↑ lower income minorities
"moving north" after
World War II. A Japanese
area earlier.

is vulnerable to development. On the southern slopes of Pacific Heights, San Francisco, the most recent rehabilitation work is in the less well maintained, minority-populated area, which is clearly vulnerable to gentrification. Similarly, in the 1940s and 1950s a lower level of maintenance in an area, along with some vacancies, "For Sale" signs, and an increasing number of poorer minority-group residents suggested vulnerability in the opposite direction. We suspect it was clues such as those that led to the massive Western Addition redevelopment projects in San Francisco—land assembly and clearance to stop a downward trend. Even though we may not feel comfortable with the actions taken, we recognize that observable clues led to these actions.

Areas in the path of perceived massive change are vulnerable, and areas that are fragile—physically, economically, or socially—are especially so. A fragile area might be one where the residents are only marginally able to maintain their properties, one where low-income residents will be the first to suffer in difficult economic times and therefore be hard put to maintain the buildings and pay the mortgages. Rapid physical deterioration is more likely if the buildings are old or in need of constant attention. Areas whose maintenance is dependent on outside subsidies such as government programs, which are vulnerable to changing political winds, are doubly vulnerable to change. In the early 1980s, we might be concerned about the future of a lower-income area like East Prescott in Oakland, which the residents have made an energetic effort to improve, but where a recently built postal service headquarters and a proposed publicly sponsored transportation center could displace some residents and make the neighborhood more vulnerable. In East Prescott, however, some clues suggest that people were organized to seek improvements through social and perhaps economic programs—notices posted of meetings, the rapid boarding up of vacant or burned properties, new walks and trees over a widespread area, of the sort that residents would be consulted on. So the area might not be as vulnerable as one would have guessed. Areas

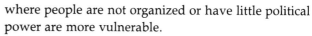

where people are not organized or have little political power are more vulnerable.

Superficial maintenance and rehabilitation, the kind of work associated with real estate speculation, can be signs of vulnerability: cheap new materials used on surfaces without attention to leakage, or foundation problems, and other, more fundamental structural matters. Large land holdings in an area where development is already occurring are more vulnerable to rapid change than are many smaller holdings, because the decisions involve fewer people.

Residential areas with sound, easily convertible buildings, standing in the path or on the fringe of healthy, expanding commercial areas, may be vulnerable to change. Commercial tenants—lawyers, doctors, professional offices, shops—can often pay higher rents than residents. On the other hand, areas where the buildings are not as sound, where the market is thin, and where there is a new or proposed change in the traffic pattern that will increase noise or speed, are vulnerable to deterioration.

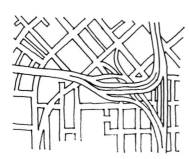

Isolated areas and those that Grady Clay calls the "seams of a city," or the no man's lands, are often subject to rapid change. Freeways and other major public works tend to be built in areas where few people live or know about, rather than where many people are active and aware. It is easier to build a major new sewage line in an industrial area than in a middle-class residential area. In San Francisco it was reasonable to expect that an overhead freeway would be built in the industrial-residential area where two distinct grid patterns come together, an area that few people can picture. In areas that people are familiar with, there would be resistance to extending the freeway. There was no resistance to a freeway in the South Bayshore area of San Francisco or to the Candlestick Park Stadium, areas that were unknown to most people.

Vulnerability to change does not mean that change will necessarily happen or, if it does, that it will be rapid. It is just as easy to mistakenly predict rapid change as to underestimate the possibility. We hear of areas that have "changed overnight," but that is not the usual case. The signs of vulnerability had probably been visible for some time if people had cared to notice. If one makes a point of observing signs of vulnerability, then there is time to check other indicators — property values, investment patterns, demographic data, the nature and speed of surrounding development — to get a sense of the imminence of change.

Questioning Change

Another way of thinking about indicators and directions of change is as a series of questions:

- Are there patterns, and if so, what are they?
- Do the patterns fit with expected patterns and processes of urban development?
- Are there new elements that break the older patterns? What is different?
- How much is new, and does it appear to be significant?
- Does the rate of change seem fast or slow?
- What do the new elements suggest about why change is taking place? Are the changes not what one would expect in that location? Are there changes from original quality or from existing conditions that suggest vulnerability to future changes?
- Is something missing? A park? A school? A place to shop?
- What kinds of additional information would help answer the questions raised by what is seen?

I am purposely suggesting that the observer keep these kinds of questions in the back of his or her consciousness. It is not useful to look too hard for problems and for change, because one may "find" something that really doesn't exist. We want to identify *existing* and *potential* change.

6 Observing the Unknown

Three major factors have attended this consideration of field observation as a tool for people who want to understand urban environments: the degree to which personal values and experience hinder objectivity, the extent to which conclusions come from fresh observations or from previously held knowledge of particular situations, and the extent to which messages taken from an urban environment are culturally bound. Even if one can usefully learn from observation in the United States, can an American read the clues in Italy or China or South America? Here I will deal with the cultural transferability of clues and more important, the transferability of the method of inquiry and diagnosis. With some surprise and more than a little satisfaction I have concluded that it is indeed possible to tell, by looking, a great deal about even a foreign city's past, evolution, present state, and dynamics. You cannot tell as much as you can about an area closer to home, but you can tell a lot.

A brief stay in China in November 1981 was the spur to some serious thinking about whether the same methods of observational inquiry can be used in a foreign culture as in our own. The clues would be different: exterior building maintenance would be less important in India or Italy, say, than in America; dress styles might be harder to decipher; one's knowledge of social and economic history, architectural styles, government, and local issues would be incomplete.

Even in the not-so-foreign environment of Charlottesville, Virginia, I mistakenly concluded that a discontinuous street pattern suggested that the development on either side of West Main Street had occurred at different times. Later I learned that the discontinuous pattern, common in the South, was meant to discourage black people from walking through white territory. Nonetheless, I started with a belief—a challenge really—that it would be possible to tell a great deal from visual clues.

In Calcutta one sees the difference between a poor area and a rich one. People drinking brownish, obviously unfiltered water from street taps or using overflowing latrines next to water sources clearly bespeak poverty and health problems. In China or Russia one can tell old buildings from new ones and estimate the sizes of the rooms inside. The size, quality, and relative newness of different spaces might not indicate the incomes of those who live in them, but they do suggest different standards. One can tell a more expensive restaurant by its appearance in China, India, or Korea, as well as in America.

I had the opportunity to spend some months in Italy in 1982; I decided to see if this method would permit the same kinds of conclusions I reached in studies done in the United States. If nothing else, the distance from my own culture might help me determine if the conclusions I was coming to at home were sound.

I tested this method in four areas in Italy: two neighborhoods in Rome; one in Bologna, and one in Milan. The areas, which were not familiar to me, were chosen by people who knew them, senior planning officials and a knowledgeable resident. The walks and observations in Rome were done right after I arrived, with very little specific knowledge of the city or of Italian history. By the time I went to Milan and Bologna two months later, I knew more. I spent from four to six hours walking around and observing each area. Then, as soon as possible, usually the same day, I presented my conclusions and interpretations to experts for confirmation. Later I consulted relevant documents to further verify my observations.[1]

Knowing about Testaccio, Rome

Testaccio is at a bend of the Tiber River in central Rome next to the Aventino area (one of the seven hills of Rome), a mile or two from the main rail terminal, a

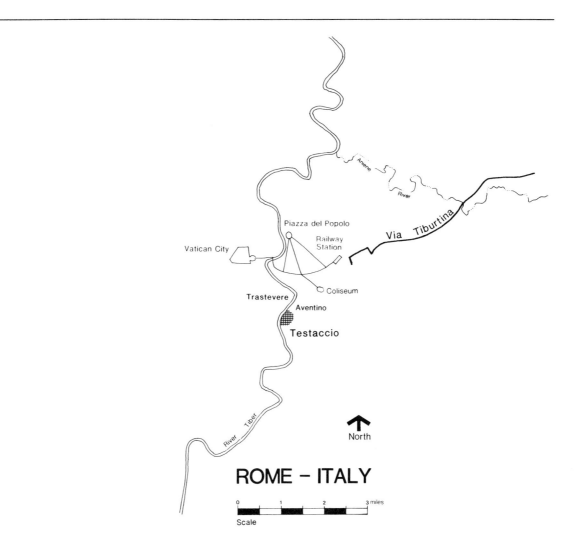

fifteen- or twenty-minute walk from the Coliseum. The
area takes its name, meaning "potsherd," from a large
hill that borders it to the south, composed of fragments
of pots and vases. It is a built-up, central city neighborhood, reasonably well defined by the river, the hill,
and a major street. It is not well known because it is
somewhat off the beaten track and has no major historic buildings (by Rome's standards) or happenings
within its bounds. Four- to six-story apartment buildings dating from the late 1800s line the streets, with
shops at street level. There is some post-World War II

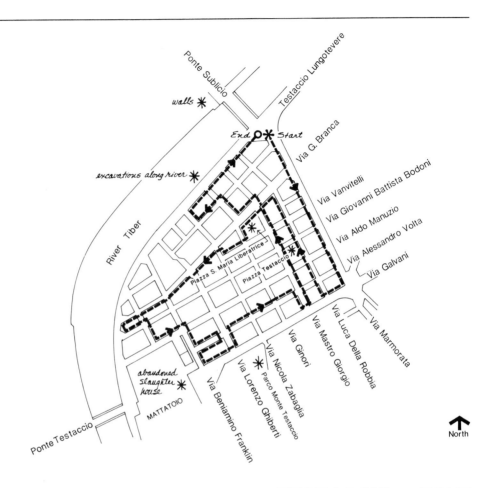

Ponte Sublicio
Testaccio Lungotevere
walls ✳
End ⚲ ✳ Start
Via G. Branca
excavations along river ✳
Via Vanvitelli
Via Giovanni Battista Bodoni
Via Aldo Manuzio
River Tiber
Via Alessandro Volta
Piazza S. Maria Liberatrice
Piazza Testaccio
Via Galvani
Via Luca Della Robbia
Via Mastro Giorgio
Via Marmorata
Via Ginori
Via Nicola Zabaglia
abandoned slaughter house ✳
Parco Monte Testaccio
Via Lorenzo Ghiberti
Via Beniamino Franklin
MATTATOIO
Ponte Testaccio

↑ North

WALKING ROUTE IN TESTACCIO – ROME

0   250   500   750   1000 feet

Scale

housing, and there are markets, churches, and an open square. The streets are busy with people and cars.

A few remnants of old walls and other ruins tell of early Roman development, and other ancient walls are visible across the river. Men are working on the old brick vaults along the river, which suggests a historic preservation project. The long, thin bricks date back to the Roman empire, if my memory from school days is correct. What existed in Testaccio in the vast period between Roman times and the late 1800s, when most of the present apartments were built?[2]

It is not easy to judge the sizes of apartments from the uniformly grand building facades, but the numbers of doorbells and nameplates, and the partitions glimpsed through windows, indicate that the units are generally small. This suggests that the area was built originally for modest-income people. The surrounding industrial uses and the low-lying elevation also suggest the same. Later I learned that the apartments originally did not have individual plumbing facilities; these were added much later. That information helped confirm my conclusion.

The apartment sizes, along with the ages, grooming, manner, and dress of the people, the types and inventories of stores, and the displayed prices are good clues to the present residents of Testaccio. Even more important was the evidence of recent maintenance and rehabilitation—newly painted buildings, new or newly varnished shutters, new finishes. Many of the people are still of modest incomes but it is a mixed area. Signs on buildings indicate that some rental units have been converted to condominiums, suggesting higher-income people. Some sections may be predominantly one income group or another, but probably there are mixes within them as well. Many older people and their families remain.

It is not easy to identify long-term physical changes in the area. To be sure, Piazza Testaccio is no longer a piazza but rather a permanent market, where the ages of food stalls and booths suggest it was established

after World War II, and there is some postwar housing. It is difficult for a foreign observer to identify changes that were part of the Fascist period—there are only two Fascist-style buildings on Via Marmorata—or to guess what the postwar housing replaced, or why.

Short-term change and present-day issues, however, are remarkably similar to what one might find in an American city, and with similar clues. There is a lot to consider. Citywide, this is a good residential location now, close to the bustling center of Rome. Earlier the area may have had a negative image because of a slaughterhouse, now abandoned, which was visible but not identified, and with lower-income housing. If there is a large demand for housing in Rome, if nearby industry is not obnoxious, and if many higher-income Europeans still like to live in city centers, then the demand for housing in Testaccio should be strong. The observed rehabilitation of housing suggests that that is the case.

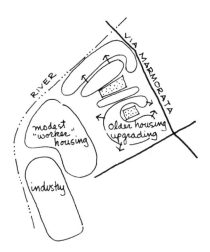

Maybe the story goes something like this: older, modest-income people have lived here in rented or owned apartments, for which there is now a strong market. There may be some kind of rent control in Italy, which owners may try to overcome by selling the units as condominiums. The area is becoming gentrified toward the north, the west, and a bit south from the market and the piazza. The level of demand differs according to location; there is less demand in the older, more modest housing to the southwest. Within buildings the level of demand is determined by the view, unit size, and accessibility.

If all this is so (as was later confirmed by a local planning official, a resident, and available historical data), then old-time moderate-income residents are probably being forced out of their apartments. But an area does not change from one income type to another overnight. Testaccio will remain a good place to live for those who can get or keep a piece of it.

Not Knowing: Tiburtina, Rome

I was much less succesful in my conclusions about a second area of Rome, along Via Tiburtina. But the walk

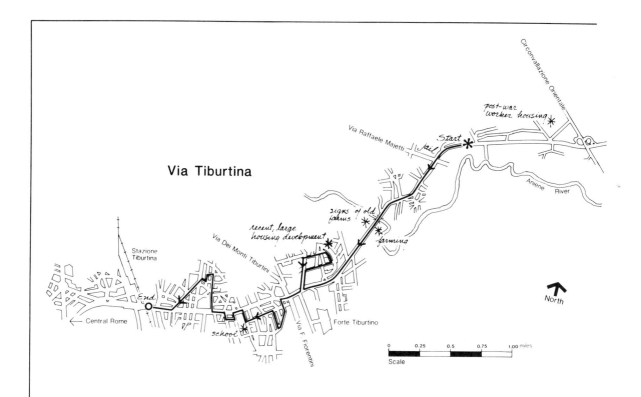

Via Tiburtina

Start

Circonvallazione Orientale

post–war worker housing

Via Raffaele Majetti

jail

Aniene River

signs of old farms

recent, large housing development

Via Dei Monti Tiburtini

farming

Stazione Tiburtina

End

← Central Rome

school

Via F. Fiorentini

Forte Tiburtino

North

Scale

0   0.25   0.5   0.75   1.00 miles

proved more instructive than Testaccio. Tiburtina is not so much an area as a long corridor, with Via Tiburtina as its spine, of urban development leading from central Rome east–northeast for some five to six miles to the city's outer ring road, the Circonvallazione Orientale, and beyond. The corridor can be viewed as a string of numerous distinct residential areas, large and small, each connected to Via Tiburtina. As one moves away from the center, the areas, which consist almost wholly of multifamily apartment houses, become newer. In 1982 considerable new development was taking place in large areas of vacant or agricultural land. The earlier post–World War II development is denser than the later, outlying housing, with a stronger orientation to Via Tiburtina, that is, with more stores and dwelling entrances directly on this street. Via Tibertina is wider, more heavily used, and more developed as one get closer to the center of Rome. It could be characterized as a Roman version of American strip development, albeit at considerably higher densities and more oriented to residential than to commercial uses. If one stops to observe five or six enclaves along the way, it can take six hours to walk the strip.

My intention was to take a bus out to the intersection of Via Tiburtina and the Circonvallazione Orientale, then walk back to the center of the city, visiting the areas along the way. But my observation did not go according to plan. Because the area through which the bus was traveling was so underdeveloped, I thought I had passed my starting point, so I got off without quite knowing where I was and started back toward the center. Later I found I had not gone as far as I should have.

I looked at most of the developed enclaves individually, as I had done in Testaccio and the American neighborhoods, though each of the Tiburtina areas was smaller and I spent less time spent in each one. The messages and the clues I took from observation were similar to those in the other cases. I could tell by and large when the area had been developed (almost all after World War II), who lived there (generally working class, not wealthy), what the residents life styles were, and even, what some emerging issues were (the need for more interior living space, better services, and solutions to traffic congestion). A great amount of new construction, mostly high-density high-rise buildings, was visible. I could see that some areas had been planned as units and that in some, public improvement programs were taking place. Most of my impressions were of separate, small areas; I learned very little about the larger area or its dynamics. My conclusions, written as notes right after the field observation, are instructive.

Clearly, Via Tiburtina is a major arterial road. I want to call it a "structural" route, one that provides structure for the metropolitan area, a road along which to organize development. What is farther out on this road—industry? jobs?

The first (farthest out) area of major new development consists of dense multifamily apartment buildings, all recent, with stores, schools, and a small central park, suggesting a planned development. The unit sizes seem small.[3] What do the residents do when they are not working? Where do they go? I expect that some of

the significant issues in the area are the lack of adequate services and facilities, such as schools, open spaces, and places for entertainment, issues that come up with so many residents in a small area. Traffic, parking, and public improvements are other likely problems.

The large amounts of vacant land between areas of development suggest that there are problems in getting access to the land for its development, in maintaining it as open space, and in knowing the traffic consequences if it is developed.

Almost all of the people in the Tiburtina areas seem to be working class; few are poor, and there are no areas of great wealth. The less affluent tend to live farther out. Closer to the center, Tiburtina becomes a less pleasant street on which to live. The traffic is heavy, and the noise is intense. But one block away from the main street, traffic is slower and there is much less noise. In these areas there may be problems in controlling growth — when and where does it end? I do not know how important these problems are felt to be.

In that brief observation my images were of many small subareas, not a whole. But there is a "whole" there, and I should have been able to see more of it. I missed the picture of Tiburtina in its historic context and as an area of long-standing social conflict and of shifting public and private development strategies.

Farther out on Via Tiburtina (thirty-one kilometers from central Rome) are Tivoli and Villa Adriana. Knowing that would have provided a clue to the fact that Via Tiburtina is a centuries-old connection between the hinterland and the city.

More immediately, I made no connection between the location and date of the large, low-income housing developments and the earlier policies of so-called slum clearance and people dislocation. If I had started farther out Tiburtina as planned, the pre–World War II low-income housing projects there would certainly have raised questions — why are they located so far out from the center? The age of that development would have placed it in the Fascist era, and I would have connected it with Mussolini's central city public works,

which involved demolitions of medieval neighbor-hoods, forcing low-income people out to these suburbs. There is a long history of poor people being forced out of European city centers. The early postwar public housing developments this far out were a continuation of these policies.

I also missed seeing a connection among the large land holdings, the locations of housing for poorer people, public improvements, and market-rate specula-tive housing closer to the center. Apparently the owners of the large holdings, which I had observed, controlled development in the area. One of them gave the city a large amount of land for public housing. I had seen the name Gerini on some buildings and institutions, but had made no inferences from it. Via Tiburtina had to be improved to get to the new housing, making the closer-in property, owned by the same people, more accessible and valuable. Once again, low-income people were forced from the center of Rome, and Tiburtina, with its access enhanced, became a great speculative area in the 1970s, starting at the railroad.

Another phenomenon I was not aware of is called "abusivismo." In the 1950s residential and industrial buildings were constructed without permits and with-out attention to local development standards. I saw examples of this unregulated development, but I did not know of its illegality, nor did I realize that the abusivismo practices were continuing. So I failed to recognize clues concerning three major types of development—public housing for poor people distant from the center, speculative development with public help, and abusivismo. To be sure, the walk started at a point where it was not possible to see some of the clues, and that is also significant.

In the 1960s and early 1970s Rome's public planners envisioned a major new employment-commercial center for much of Rome in this general area. The plans involved building new residential areas in the agricul-tural lands, clearing and redeveloping the ancient areas and the abusivismo, and creating a system of parks along the river to separate housing from industry. Most of this was not done. I did not realize that the mix of old and new development was part of a more recent, conscious plan to legalize what had been illegal, adding needed public works, parks, streets, and services, and building new public housing. There is a conscious policy to achieve a mix of incomes within areas and to lower the population densities in high-density residential areas so that services can be provided.

Why did I miss so much? There are many instructive explanations, not the least of which was the shift in geographic scale. A sense of the big picture does not always evolve from putting together small, observable pieces. Window grilles, recent maintenance and rehabilitation, apartments expanding to include balconies as living space, trees, and store prices may tell about the dynamics of a particular area, but to get the larger view one must consider the patterns of an extended area, say the concentration of low-income housing at one location, compared with other types of housing at different locations. It is important to be aware of scale, to look at both the large and the small. In this case I had not realized that the appropriate scale for interpreting had changed.

There is always some element that an observer cannot see. In the case of Tiburtina the early, low-income housing estates that signaled early public policies and action were just beyond the point where my observation started. The physical clues that could help an observer understand will be physically distant, beyond hope of being seen even in twenty field excursions. If public policies—a proposal for a new employment-commercial center or a park or the demolition of abusivismo—have not been carried out, there will be no clues.

From the start I have said that case studies cannot be true reflections of how field observation works in practice. Tiburtina reminds us of the importance of the iterative, back and forth nature of observation over time and in combination with other research methods. Tiburtina underlines the importance of relating what is seen to social-economic and political-historical contexts. An observer who knows the political history of the country would have insights that a less knowledgeable observer might miss. An outsider may see something new, make some new associations that escape the local observer, but the outsider cannot know the socio-political history as well as someone immersed in that culture.

Observation is not a test; its goal is not just conclusions but questions. In Tiburtina, I did not ask enough questions, at least not consciously, perhaps because I tried to see so much in a relatively short period and to take it all in. Instead of continually questioning what I was seeing and relating the observed environment to my knowledge of other cities, I was in a rush to simply observe. If the Tiburtina case has a failing, it is in not ending up with enough questions.

Knowing a Bit More: Bologna

Bologna was as unfamiliar to me as Testaccio and Tiburtina had been, but by the time I observed Bologna I had been in Italy for eight weeks.[4] Just that amount of time helped me understand what to look for in Italian cities. Then too, I had learned from the two Rome cases.

The area of Bologna I walked in, called Mazzini, is larger than Testaccio and much smaller than the Tiburtina. It is removed from the city center by a bus ride of approximately twenty minutes. Mazzini straddles two main roads leading from the center of the city and could be likened to two or three of the larger individual housing areas on either side of Via Tiburtina. There is both older and recent development, largely residential, with commercial concentrations and some smaller industrial uses mixed in.

Imagine that we have just come to Bologna and are about to spend some time observing an unknown area. Bologna is in the highly industrialized and productive north of Italy, where the people are said to have a high standard of living and the food is supposed to be as fine as can be found in Italy. We know that the people of Bologna have voted for a Communist administration for the last thirty-six years or so, but we do not know how this will affect what we see. We know there is a city policy to limit the population to approximately

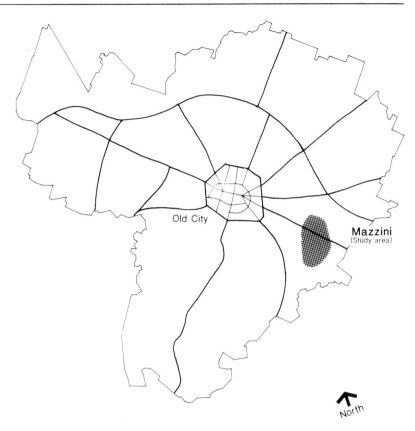

BOLOGNA – ITALY

Scale

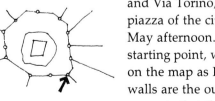

600,000, presumably to avoid sprawl, and to preserve and restore old buildings without dislocating the residents. The building restoration work in the city center very carefully reflects the original designs and is said to be costly.

We begin our walk at the corner of Via Degli Ortolani and Via Torino, more than two miles from the central piazza of the city. It is about three o'clock on a warm May afternoon. It has been raining. On the way to our starting point, we saw city walls and a gate, identified on the map as Porta Santo Stefano. We assume these walls are the outermost ring of three; the road pattern suggests that there might have been two other sets of walls. Something else on the map that catches our eye

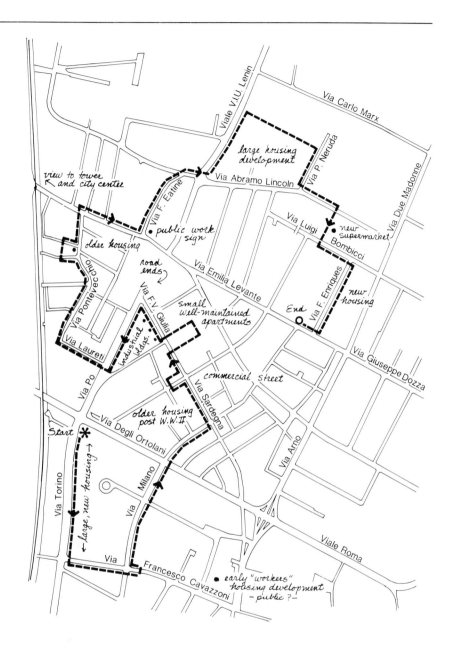

WALKING ROUTE IN BOLOGNA – ITALY

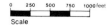

Scale

North

is the evenly spaced grid pattern of other roads and lines, covering at least the eastern part of the city. Via Emilia, Via Degli Ortolani, Via Po, and Via Arno are pieces of that grid in the area where we will walk. Is this grid part of an earlier city plan? It seems unrelated to anything else we see.

Walking south on Via Torino, we see large housing blocks that appear to have been built within the last ten years. Housing like this in the United States would probably be publicly subsidized. The finishing materials are not of particularly high quality, and the grounds maintenance leaves something to be desired. The buildings are set back from the street, oriented to auto use, with large parking lots. The buildings are widely spaced.

The buildings to the south of Via Francesco Cavazzoni on the extension of Via Torino are a bit older, as are the trees. The buildings are somewhat smaller and closer to the street; the quality of materials and finishes looks better; the building arrangements are tighter and closer together. The street seems more of a piece. The building at the corner has two or three shops.

In a large building on the north side of Via Cavazzoni some units have converted the balconies to interior rooms to enlarge the living space. These conversions may indicate that the units are privately owned condominiums. This housing is more complex in design than the first group. Further along on Via Cavazzoni, it is clear that the landscaping is older than that to the north. There is a shopping strip on the south side. Some teenagers play cards at a table outdoors.

Moving north on Via Milano, we see a number of housing developments with different sizes of buildings on varying amounts of ground. One senses some tension or indecision among the architects as to whether or not to orient buildings to the street. Some three-story houses on the east side of Via Milano are brand new. Across Via Ortolani at Via Calabria are smaller, older free-standing apartment blocks with greater land coverage than we have seen to this point. They date from after World War II.

The street system here is a grid that does not parallel

the four defining streets of the grid we saw on the map. Why? Storm windows have been added to some of the units, and some buildings have been repainted. The housing looks as if it had all been built in the 1950s; the different colors and details suggest that the units are privately owned. Maintenance is uniformly adequate. There is less off-street parking than there is south of Via Ortolani. At one point the trees are *in* the street, an indication that the residents valued the trees enough to insist on saving them when the street was widened. The cracks in the street may indicate where the curbs used to be. New trees have been planted to replace older ones that have been cut down. More people are out on the street here than we saw earlier.

Along Via Sardegna the buildings have colonnades, as in older sections of Bologna, although this development seems to be postwar. The stores sell utilitarian goods; there are no stylish displays, nothing high fashion, much like the store inventories in an area of Milan. In America these kinds of stores would be associated with a lower-middle-income area. Most of the stores we see are small. Are they large enough to generate a reasonable income? The people here are of all ages. Older men are playing cards in just about every bar. Around the Piazza Belluno the housing is larger and newer.

Three small industrial buildings, all built after World War II, line one side of Via Friuli-Venezia Giulia. They house a BMW auto shop, a Peugeot auto shop, and one

or two small industries. Why are they here? The last building, at the end of the street, has a section that rises above the rest with apartments in it. This building is not as well maintained as the others. Perhaps the realization of the idea of working and living in the same building did not work out too well.

The apartment buildings on the narrower side streets off Via Friuli-Venezia Giulia, though not new, are well maintained, newly painted, with new windows and doors and some new balconies.

Via Po looks as though it was intended to be a main street, has had recent construction work, but it ends abruptly, blocked by a building. Does the road continue on the other side? Steps lead down from Via Po to Via Laureti, a lovely dead-end street. Some of the housing here is pre–World War II, but it has been rehabilitated. There is a mix of building sizes, scales, types, and ages. Since the street is close to a railroad line, it was probably not considered a choice location even as late as the 1950s. When was the railroad electrified, with less dirt and noise? What effect did that have on nearby properties? The older industrial uses along the rail line may be related to the industries we saw on Via Frioli-Venezia Giulia.

In the Via Pontevecchio area some housing seems to be as old as the turn of the century, but it is all in good condition. The streets are narrower and more irregular; some have recently been repaved. There is considerable new in-fill housing. The new houses are painted in the same few colors—ocher, orange, sienna—we have seen all over the city. What do the many "Strada Privata" signs mean? Some of the older housing is substantial in size, suggesting that the original owners were well to do.

We sense thus far a strong public presence and involvement throughout the area, in the housing on Via Torino, the concentrated rehabilitation of older buildings, the colors. But we do not know how much or what kinds.

The people we see on the streets look like industrial workers, decidedly not people who work in offices. They are wearing "work clothes," not jackets or stylish dresses. It is now 5:20 P.M., so perhaps the office workers have not yet come home.

Via Emilia Levante looks like an older main street, and a look at the map confirms that it is a main radial leading out from what must have been another city gate. Where does it go? In Milan we concluded that a similar road was an old radial route leading from Como or Varese to a city wall or gate. Looking toward town, we see a very tall, very old tower.

Along Via Emilia the shops tend to be higher style; the clothes are stylish and elegantly displayed, the furniture is contemporary. There is a lot of traffic.

A sign says that the city is renovating an old villa, converting it to a public use. The sign contains considerable financial information about the project. At Via Lincoln and Via Lenin is another area of very large, new housing estates set in open space. Are they public or private or a mix? A private developer probably would not have named a street for Lenin. Other street names: Via Allende, Via Marx.

The people here seem more fashionably dressed. A mother and her young son wear matching colors and styles. The teenagers circulate in groups more than we've seen elsewhere. How easy is it for older people—and teenagers—to meet casually and talk with one another? The big open spaces and the orientation of buildings away from streets raises the question. Maybe that is our selective vision at work. It is a development that one would expect to drive to more easily than walk.

One private housing development (presumed from a sign saying "condominio") has some public uses—a nursery school, a school, and other social institutions. What is the disctinction here between public and private? We have not seen any stores in the area. With

this kind of housing, we expect an American-style shopping center with a parking lot, and sure enough, as we turn a corner, we see Supermercato. Walking to the shopping center, we are aware for the first time of being disoriented; we do not know what direction we are walking in in relation to the main streets or to downtown.

In the Supermercato parking area there are cars in most of the stalls. By American standards the enclosed mall is small, and at 6:10 it is not very crowded. The merchandise in the stores appears to be of a bit better quality than on Via Sardegna but is not high style.

As we walk toward Via Emilia, we see new buildings, and the smell of fresh concrete is in the air. Where have the new residents come from? Most of the cars are small, and most of the license plates indicate Bologna.

At Via Emilia it starts to rain again. We get on a bus for the eighteen-minute ride to the center of the city. It is interesting that at this time of the evening the bus gets more crowded as it moves toward the center; that would not be the case in the United States.

To summarize our observations, it seems reasonable to conclude that Via Emilia, running through the center of the area, has been a major route into the city for a long, long time. It focuses on an old city gate; it may have been a route that brought food and goods to the city markets. A main rail line parallels Emilia. We have not learned the meaning of the street grid we identified at the start of the walk, but we cannot help thinking it represents some early planning effort.

The age of the buildings suggests that there was very little development in the area before World War II. The land may have been owned by farmers with large acreages and by a few people with villas. There was also some industrial development near the railroad. After World War II came the housing at Via Sardegna and that closer to the railroad. There seems to have been a long history of public planning and direct action in the area, perhaps associated with "saving" the city center, but we cannot be confident about that connection.

The area bounded by Via Po, Via Emilia, Via Arno, and Via Ortolani was probably one of the first to be

developed with some public involvement after the war. The regularity of the streets in this area, the colonnades at Via Sardegna, and the extensive private and public maintenance suggest a public role in some form — direct public action, regulation, coercion, or what?

Development to the south and north of this older core (the beginning and end of the walk) is on a much larger scale, and it looks almost as if the city planners decided to make a much larger, faster effort to attain their citywide housing and population objectives. The public role seems similar to redevelopment in the United States, where the government expropriates the land, then sells some of it to private developers to be designed and built according to a plan and develops some of it directly for public purposes, including subsidized housing. We assume, because of the Communist city administration that the government role is more important here than in America.

Checking with Reality

Immediately following the field observation, I met with a Bologna city planner and former government official, Giuseppe Campos Venuti, who had been intimately involved with the city's planning and development for many years, including the efforts in the observed area.

Via Emilia is indeed old, over 2,000 years old, part of a Roman road over the Apennines, a military route linking Roman towns in the region. It existed even before the Roman era.

The street grid we identified also dates back to Roman times. The Romans divided the land into a grid, called *centuriatio*, with roads running parallel and perpendicular to Via Emilia. Roman soldiers who married local women and who agreed to care for the land were given all or part of a square, thereby keeping the new lands under Roman control. Though large parts of the grid have been destroyed over the years, some remain as property divisions, marked by irrigation channels, streets, and storm sewers. Thus the old remains visible. There were only two sets of walls, not three; the original Roman walls were totally destroyed. The railroad, built in the late 1800s, runs parallel to Via

Emilia because it was intended to make the same connections.

Our observations about development after World War II were largely correct. Development was rapid and in some places (near the railroad) haphazard, as we thought. The central area between Via Ortolani and Via Emilia was largely developed by 1960, but there was little or no direct public involvement in the building process. Up until 1960 the planning philosophy was to place public, subsidized housing on the outskirts of town to the east, in a large concentrated development just beyond the area we observed (the same problem that occurred in Tiburtina).[5] In the old European tradition, low-income housing was put on the fringe of the city. Following World War II the fashion was to tear down and rebuild much of the old city core, not unlike programs then in operation in the United States. In 1960 the left-wing administration changed the policy radically; urban planning and development became a basic focus for the new leaders. One main objective was to achieve a mix of incomes and occupations throughout the city to avoid divisions by class. Working-class people were to live in all areas, not segregated on the outskirts. In the area we observed, since its center was already built, the plan was to reserve the area north of Via Emilia and south of Via Ortolani for the working class. Thus public housing was built in the area between Via Ortolani and Via Cavazzoni, as we observed, and the land south of Via Cavazzoni, developed first, was done privately.[6] The unlandscaped areas in the public area are not finished, which accounts for their somewhat unkempt condition. The private housing here is at a higher density than the public housing, presumably to encourage private developers. The city bought only the land it used for building the public housing and services.

The policy in Milan was similar. There my misperceptions about Tiburtina helped sharpen the visual inquiry, and I realized that new public services — schools, athletic facilities, some housing — might be part of a planning strategy to facilitate a mix of older and newer residents as well as people with different incomes. There, too, street improvements in abusivismo areas were part of the strategy of economic-social integration, as in Tiburtina and Bologna.

In Bologna, the area north of Via Emilia is a mix of public and private development: two "islands" of land within the larger area were left for private development according to public standards and controls. Private and public construction have been simultaneous. Apparently, our concern about the suitability of the area for older people was misplaced; they express happiness with their new environment. At another time of day or on weekends, we might have seen many more people in the new areas. Most of the new residents living in this area come from the Bologna region. The observation about the central area being largely working class was also correct.

In the central area of our walk, city policy has been to equalize some differences among people by bringing the area between Via Ortolani and Via Emilia up to par with the newly developed areas. Housing density has been reduced, services added, and the amount of new development severely limited. Since a recent city law discourages demolition of older buildings, residents now feel they own or live in something of value, so there is much private rehabilitation. Those who live in modest, fifty-year-old housing built for workers on the outskirts of town now are surrounded by more contemporary structures, new housing and services. As a consequence, they may feel that they are more of an integral part of the community.

The local experts told me that the small industrial area and the factory were an experiment in living and working in the same place, as we had guessed. Industry did not use the railroad but was located there because the land was cheap. The owners of houses built during the period of spontaneous growth were later required to pay two-thirds of the costs of streets, walks, and the like, so they put up the "Strada Privata" signs. Private developers had at first rejected the proposal to build the shopping center, so the city urged cooperatives to build it, and they are doing quite well financially.

On the whole, the field observation and analysis

were reasonably correct, guided of course by a new familiarity with the country and the earlier cases. To be sure, there were errors and misperceptions. Clues that might indicate certain problems in the United States— an unfinished road improvement, for example—in Bologna only meant that the government was waiting to purchase a building that was in the way. The Italian urban political history associated with geographical location went largely unnoticed.[7] Nevertheless, the development history of the outskirts of one major city is not likely to be very different from that of another in the same region. And the political, planning, and development strategies of different cities are likely to be similar in any recent period because the planners are all responding to similar economic, social, and political forces, and they communicate with and learn from one another.

Learning from the Unknown

Clearly, the meanings of some observable physical clues found in urban environments are the same from one culture to another. Some clues seem to be more universal and useful than others. For centuries, bars and grilles over doors and windows have been a response to safety problems. In any culture certain features of buildings reveal relative wealth or stature of the residents. Some characteristics of residents—sex, age, sometimes dress—have similar meanings regardless of where they are. Nameplates, doorbells, signs, dates on buildings, numbers of floors, and sizes of units are always useful clues. Other clues, such as topographic elevation in relation to wealth, diversity of building styles, location of homes in relation to sunlight may be almost universally applicable. Street and building layouts and juxtapositions of land uses can tell the extent of central planning. The Italian studies confirm that the types of goods sold in stores can indicate the income-employment status of the residents.

But it is not my intention to review individual clues for their universality of application. The question is not whether a clue has the same meaning everywhere, but whether it is usable in its context. It is the way one looks at clues and uses them that transcends cultural differences. We look for *relationships* between clues. In Testaccio the size of the buildings (small), the location of the area in the city (low-lying, at a bend in the river), and the surrounding industrial uses (former slaughterhouse) taken together suggest a low-income area. People's clothing and the merchandise in local stores helped confirm that impression in Testaccio as well as in parts of the Bologna neighborhood.

In Italy, as in America, *patterns* of clues and their *relative newness* can be more important than the clues themselves: an area of new window shutters or newly painted buildings in Testaccio; a pattern of many small single-family houses of slightly different designs on small lots and narrow but very regular streets, which indicates abusivismo in Milan; areas of massive new public and private construction in Tiburtina and Bologna, signs of public policies.

Finally, the way of looking and the way of questioning are important. The questions are the same as those we would ask in a familiar environment. They have to do with being aware of what we see, identifying patterns in relation to known historic processes of urban development, asking why things are the way they are, gauging the amounts and pace of change, wondering if anything is missing, considering what it is like to live in the area, and asking if what is seen tells anything about the larger urban context.

The major problem, as the Italian studies showed, is that an observer does not usually know the historic context of a foreign culture, either generally or in relation to a particular urban area. These Italian observations point to the importance of seeing the environment in relation to understood economic-political periods.

Also, it is important to understand that space and building norms and standards are likely to vary greatly among cultures and over time. In Tiburtina I assumed that the space standards for publicly assisted housing would be less than in the United States and that families were still quite large. Later I learned that in the early 1980s space standards for publicly assisted units in Italy are higher than in the United States and that family sizes in the cities have dropped almost as abruptly as in this country. It would not have been difficult to measure unit sizes in Tiburtina to get a better knowledge of sizes.

Notwithstanding the errors of the Italian observations, it was encouraging to find out how fast one learns by observation. The misperceptions and omissions of Tiburtina, once explained, helped me recognize some of the history, development patterns, public planning strategies, and even detailed designs of Bologna, and later Milan. Once I learned about development strategies under the Fascists before World War II and under the postwar governments, I was able to understand some patterns in Bologna and Milan. I recognized abusivismo once the practice had been explained. Knowing about the present-day strategy in Rome of consciously mixing income groups and of concentrating public facilities and services where they can be an integrating force made it possible to recognize these policies elsewhere.

There is an unanticipated dividend to these kinds of experimental case studies. Consider what happens: you, an outsider, spend a few hours walking through part of a city, and then you proceed to tell a local official, who has probably lived in the area for years about its history, people, and possibly some problems. Even if you are correct in the observations and conclusions, you are bound to miss a lot. The expert, the person who *knows,* ends up desiring to tell you not only where you were right or wrong, but also what you missed, including a lot of political history. Your diagnosis can let loose a flood of information, particularly because your hypotheses and conclusions are of interest to the local expert. You tell the expert about his or her city; the expert is amazed at and humored by the attempt and quickly opens up with all kinds of information that would not have been forthcoming otherwise. Thus the context of learning and teaching is one of good humor. Without fail, this was the case in Italy. What a happy, fast way to learn about a city!

7 Looking Back

As parents always say to their children, "It's in front of you. Use your eyes." We take messages—or we fail to take them—from urban environments by looking, and we act upon those messages to maintain or change or create places in ways that seem appropriate responses to urban problems and opportunities.

This book calls for getting involved with what we see: learning from what we observe in the urban environment; employing observation more consciously and regularly as an analytic and decision-making tool; and using what we learn to help people live in concert with one another and with the land. If conscious, systematic observation, as opposed to haphazard visual experiencing, does nothing more than help avoid unfortunate decisions and actions that affect people's lives, it will have served well. But it can do much more than that.

I want to summarize briefly some of the more significant findings about observation and to offer additional ideas that can help any interested city dweller go out and do it. There is nothing quite like walking as a way to observe and get to know a city. Much more than any other mode of transportation, walking allows the observer to control the pace of observation, and there are fewer distractions than there are when driving or riding a bike. It is possible to get to otherwise inaccessible places. Most important, walking allows the observer to be in the environment more fully, and the deliberate pace permits one to integrate what is seen with the knowledge and experiences stored in one's mind. I also think it facilitates recall.

There are problems, to be sure, not the least of which is that the observer feels like an intruder in an unfamiliar environment and therefore is uncomfortable.

Because of that feeling, the observer may see things differently, may look too rapidly, may come to conclusions that reflect the discomfort. Women, who can be targets of overt observation, verbal confrontation, and sometimes even physical abuse, are more likely to be uncomfortable as walking observers, a problem that has yet to be overcome. A short, simple explanation of what one is doing can be an adequate response to the "Who are you? What are you doing here?" questions, even when asked with hostility. Once people know what the observer is doing, they are often pleased to talk about or show their neighborhoods.

For some purposes and at certain scales, walking may not be appropriate. A helicopter trip is a good way to find out quickly where major new development is happening or is likely to happen in the future. One flight over the Phoenix area clearly shows that nothing will stop the development of all the presently cultivated land, and maybe more, if someone wants to do so. Donald Appleyard and Kevin Lynch reconnoitered all of the San Diego metropolitan area in one afternoon by helicopter, and the messages they read became an important part of their subsequent work there.[1]

Low-density suburban areas, which were designed for driving, not walking, invite observation by car. The windshield survey has its uses, particularly for getting a general impression of the nature of development and the income status of residents. But I would always suggest getting out of the car at some point and taking a walk, even if only for ten minutes. One begins to experience the area differently.

Buses and other public transportation, bicycle, boat — all can be appropriate for specific purposes. When walking is not possible or appropriate, one should look for clues that are consistent with the speed of looking and the distance from what is being looked at. In a car or helicopter, for example, one should not try to see or interpret detail. Look for the physical qualities of large areas, not the dynamics within them.

Do not try to take photos and observe at the same time. Taking a picture interrupts observing and thinking about and questioning what you see. The photographer is concerned with focus, lens openings, composition, light, and shadow, with how the picture will look. Come back to take pictures later.

Sketching, however, helps looking, makes one more observant. One can think about what one is seeing while sketching, how the elements are arranged and fit together. Sketching facilitates measuring, which, as I have noted, is crucial in making comparisons and understanding the meaning of small and large, good and bad, a lot and a little. Drawing skills are not important, because the sketch will not be shown to anyone.

If possible, walk an area at a time when it is busy. Seeing more people means seeing more clues, and also seeing how people use their city, what is important to them and what is less so. At the same time, the observer should be aware that this is an active time and should try to imagine what it is like at other times. An area may have a very different character in summer and winter, sun and rain, day and night. Understanding these differences is the next best thing to repeated and prolonged observation.

There is no best path, no best place to start or stop a walk. If there is a best way, it is to follow a number of different, overlapping paths, including those that go in back of buildings, along alleys and service lanes. Backs sometimes tell more about maintenance, condition, and space than fronts. People are always surprised at the spaciousness of rear yards in many densely populated eastern cities and in San Francisco.

In this business of looking and interpreting, two people seem to be better than one. Two people can question each other, develop and challenge more hypotheses, bring more knowledge to a situation. Two people may also be an answer to the safety problem women face when alone in some areas. If there is a drawback to having two or more observers, it is that it takes more time to express verbally what one is seeing or thinking, and in that time the observer is less aware of the environment.

When I am observing, I talk with anyone who speaks to me in a friendly way or who, after eye contact and a nod or smile, seems willing to talk. Firemen at leisure, storekeepers, real estate brokers, and librarians know a lot about their areas; so may a person walking along the street. The observer uses everything he can get his hands on to understand and plan for a community; the residents are a very good source of information.

Remember that observation is not a test. No one is forcing the observer to come up with conclusions, except perhaps himself. Don't try to cover too much ground at one time, because one sees less when tired.

A single clue cannot answer questions about an area's historic development and evolution, present state, and problems that exist or may unfold. Taken together, clues are more meaningful, but even then their meanings are more "iffy" than precise. That iffiness is not necessarily a problem; it is a reality that is also true of other research and diagnostic techniques. The lack of certainty may lead to a number of alternative hypotheses about an area, which can be tested if they are important enough. Rather than being a problem, the unsureness of observation makes an area more real, alive, breathing.

Observers see things differently, even to the extent of seeing different clues. But it should come as no surprise that any number of different clues may lead one to similar conclusions about an area. Seeing a rash of bicycles, basketball hoops, caution signs for drivers, all within a tract of ten-year-old three-bedroom homes may lead an observer to conclude that there are many school-aged children, that the families have a particular life style, and even that certain problems will accompany this population group. But an observer who sees none of those clues but sees a neighborhood school with many students might well come to the same conclusions. In a follow-up observation of the Naglee Park area, two relatively inexperienced observers came to conclusions that were remarkably consistent with those reported in Chapter 2, although both their walking route and many of their clues were different. The point is, one need have no fear of not seeing "the right things"—there may be no right things. There is plenty to see, plenty from which to take messages and form hypotheses.

The knowledge one brings to observation can help narrow down the many possible interpretations of what is seen. What knowledge is most helpful? The *social and economic history* of a culture and urban area is crucial; that knowledge is the context for what is observed. When did important social and economic movements take place? What was life like for people here in different periods? What was the timing of reform movements? How have welfare concepts and programs, government roles, technology, and political movements and philosophies changed over time? This knowledge is just as important locally as on a regional or national scale.

Urban planners and others involved in city conservation and development should know *how cities have grown and developed physically.* They should be able to relate that knowledge to the social and economic history of the culture. One ought to know, for example, how streetcars and railroads and highways have structured city development.

Some knowledge of *architectural styles* and their history is important. Experience suggests that to be useful, style periods need not be precise and that they can be longer the further removed they are from the present day: pre–Civil War, late 1800s, turn of the century, the 1920s, the Depression, pre-World War II, 1950s, 1960s, post-1960s. Most people know more than they think they do about when different styles of buildings were constructed. Without studying the subject, however, they are not likely to know enough to consistently understand what these styles tell us about urban areas.

In the same way, knowledge of *artifact history* is profoundly useful. By this I mean the time periods when different types of curbs, street lights, paving materials, signs, curtains, blinds, and building materials were used. This knowledge is more difficult to acquire; there are so many details, and the evolution of any one kind is rarely documented or easily discovered. Reading old photographic journals and technical manuals and looking for dates on the artifacts themselves helps. Perhaps more than for any other category of clues, this

information is best learned from experienced professionals. Once a person becomes aware of and starts
thinking about the history of a detail, say of the different kinds of curbs that have been used in a city, it
becomes an enjoyable pastime to find out more about it.

It is critical to know something of *construction* and
maintenance. The condition and maintenance of buildings are important clues to problems and changes that
are taking place. Nonspecialist observers often do not
understand building construction and what it takes to
keep a building in good condition. This can be learned,
if not from taking academic courses then from reading
books and manuals on construction and renovation,
from being a truly attentive sidewalk superintendent at
construction sites, or from actually building and maintaining a house.[2]

Almost all of this knowledge can be learned. Effective
observation and diagnosis require no special gift, but
they are facilitated by all the knowledge one has accumulated and by constant conscious questioning of what
is observed.

The next question is, what can you do with what you
find out by looking? There are situations where observation may be the only tool available to suggest what
to do. A group or an official or a potential client may
need to know quickly how to go about planning for a
specific area. There may be only enough time for one
site visit before making some initial decisions. I was
once told by the officials of a large city that they were
strongly considering a major development project,
which they would be announcing soon. What did I
think about their intentions? In the two to three hours I
spent in the area I came up with what seemed *obvious*
questions about dislocation of people and businesses,
traffic circulation, the market for what they were considering, and more. Some of those questions had not
been obvious to the officials; at least they had not
thought about them. They decided to find out a great
deal more about the area before proceeding.

Usually observation is used, less dramatically, with
other research tools in a continuous, back and forth
manner. Today a team of observers recognizes that

downtown seems to be pushing into a neighboring residential area. This observation generates economic and demographic research, with implications for public policies and programs. Tomorrow some traffic data calls for a field trip to see what the actual conditions are like. Often the local residents' concerns about a particular issue generate coordinated research, including observation. In any case, field observation is used along with other research methods.

Early knowledge of a problem permits early action, if that is appropriate, or early preparation for action. Observation may reduce the number of surprises to be faced. If one knows by looking that a large unused railroad yard near a busy downtown area is a likely site for development, then one can prepare for it. After looking at an area south of San Francisco's downtown, an area of marginal economic uses and boardinghouses for poor, transient men, I was able to advise a potential purchaser of land for a small new office building that the location was presently inappropriate. But having also seen signs that the downtown area was rapidly expanding in that direction, I was also able to advise the buyer that depending on the price and the length of time he could hold an empty lot, the site would soon have potential value for what he had in mind.

Observation also enables planners to take early direct action in response to problems and opportunities. In 1968, toward the end of the Johnson administration in Washington, San Francisco had an unexpected opportunity to receive federal funds for small, neighborhood parks. Within thirty days the city would have to propose specific sites where the money could be appropriately used. Intimate knowledge of the city, gained in large measure through looking, enabled a handful of staff to come up with over a hundred sites almost overnight, from which the final thirty-three locations were then chosen.[3]

The city is the first line of government for most of the people who live there. They experience their joys as well as their problems and frustrations where they live and work, and it is there that they state their expectations and lodge their complaints. Cities are people's homes as much as the more limited series of private rooms that we usually call "home." The city is the public home, the focus of our collective existence.

More than at any other level of government, the city is where the action is. Actions, whether planned or unplanned, take place within a context of specific faces, names, and places. Anyone concerned with potential changes in an urban fabric will relate abstract policies and plans to tangible experiences. The professional planners, active citizens, and those who want to better understand their society, can see and experience what they are dealing with at the city scale.

I think also that any meaningful plan for a city, including small building projects, should start with an *understanding* of the nature of the place and should call for respecting and improving the existing physical character of the community. It should respond to important social and economic issues within that framework.

To a considerable extent, this book has been about becoming more aware of our communities so that we may respond more knowingly to issues and opportunities. It is also about becoming aware of the messages we may take from observed environments and of making positive use of the knowledge gained. It calls attention to a neglected but universally available and inexpensive tool, our eyes, that can be used so easily with another tool, our minds, by the simple process of going out into the community.

To me it seems reasonable that people who want to change a city by responding to physical or socioeconomic problems or who have certain utopian ideals in mind would be enthralled by the physical aspect of the city and would want to spend as much time in it as possible. But that does not seem to be the case. I am not sure why, but people do not seem to observe cities directly very much. Perhaps information gained from the environment directly seems less safe and sure than more easily manipulated statistical sources. Perhaps people just do not know how to look or how to take messages (even though they are unconsciously doing so). I hope this book has helped overcome some of those problems and has shown that looking can be creative and fun. Newness, discovery, surprise, empathy, anticipation of what is coming, wondering about what is, what was, and how it all happened, being filled with what the eyes take in and then mulling over all those images, pushing the eye-mind relationships to the hilt, wanting to go back and see more — certainly that is fun.

In the end, the whole process of looking, questioning, trying to gain understanding makes a person a more intimate, repectful part of any environment and therefore more likely to be caring of it. That is the basis for good planning and beneficial action.

Notes

1. Starting to Look

1. In all the case studies I attempt to describe the sequence of what comes to the observer's eye, understanding that this cannot literally be done. It is an attempt to combine the visual impressions that are perceived as possibly important, which implies initial judgments and a sifting out, with a judgment of how best to communicate to a reader in a way that is likely to be understood.

2. Vinson Brown, *Reading the Woods* (New York: Collier Books, 1969).

3. Peirce F. Lewis, "Axioms for Reading the Landscape," in *The Interpretation of Ordinary Landscapes: Geographical Essays,* ed. D. W. Meining (New York: Oxford University Press, 1979).

4. Grady Clay, *Close-up: How to Read the American City* (New York: Praeger, 1973).

5. See, for example, Anthony J. Cantonese and James C. Snyder, eds., *Introduction to Urban Planning* (New York: McGraw-Hill, 1979), p. 153.

6. Arthur D. Little, Inc., *San Francisco Community Renewal Program* (Final Report to City Planning Commission, City and County of San Francisco, California, October 1965).

7. M. L. Johnson Abercrombie, *The Anatomy of Judgement; An Investigation into the Process of Perception and Reasoning* (New York: Basic Books, 1960) p. 58.

8. L. Jacoby, "Perception of Air, Noise and Water Pollution in Detroit" (Michigan Geographical Publication no. 7, Department of Geography, University of Michigan, Ann Arbor, 1972).

9. Roger M. Downs and David Stea, eds., *Image and Environment* (Chicago: Aldine, 1973), p. xii.

10. William H. Ittelson, *An Introduction to Environmental Psychology* (New York: Holt, Rinehart and Winston, 1974), p. 13.

11. William H. Ittelson, *Environment and Cognition* (New York: Seminar Press, 1973), pp. 13–15.

2. Observing and Interpreting Naglee Park

1. Leslie Gould and I carried out this case study, assisted by Julia Gould
and Janet Linse, who arranged the field trip with staff of the City Planning Department of San Jose and who assembled data from which we assessed the observation. The study was first published as "Observing and Interpreting the Urban Environment: Naglee Park, San Jose, California" (Working Paper no. 372, Institute of Urban and Regional Development, University of California, Berkeley, February 1982).

2. Redlining refers to a bank's decision that because property values in an area are decreasing, loans there are to be considered a high risk. The area is outlined in red on the bank's maps.

3. We also tested the tentative conclusions we reached in the field against published reports of the planning department, census materials, and newspaper articles. As with other case studies, it was difficult to verify our conclusions; the necessary data were just not available, even though we chose the area because the city planning staff had asserted that studies of it existed.

4. Having observed that Naglee Park is close to downtown, the observers failed to speculate about what this might have meant for the area's development over time.

3. Clues

1. Carl Bernstein and Bob Woodward, *All the President's Men* (New York: Simon and Schuster, 1974), p. 82.

2. For a particularly astute series of observations about development that gets larger in scale at every stage, see Grady Clay, *Close-Up: How to Read the American City* (New York: Praeger, 1973), p. 88.

3. For example, in San Francisco, tall buildings built after 1972 have less floor space per floor than those of other cities because of a bulk ordinance passed as part of an urban design plan.

4. See Robert Cassidy, "San Francisco Fights to Save Face," *Planning* (June 1973), concerning how some officials of the Department of Housing and Urban Development viewed the physical conditions of San Francisco's Bernal Heights area.

5. The products might be substantially different, but the example would apply to large-scale, *designed* public housing in the United States or to designed housing developments in socialist countries.

6. The greater wealth may be in the form of a public decision to spend resources to maintain property at a certain level, that is, to publicly subsidize private property, thereby indicating community values.

7. Berkeley Planning Associates, *Recommended Policy and Program Options for San Francisco: An Anti-Displacement Strategy* (Berkeley, 1980).

8. When I was traveling from northern to southern Switzerland for the first time, via one of their very long tunnels, I said to my companion when we emerged, "Ah, we're in a different country, maybe Italy." I explained that the land was less neatly tended, more things were lying around at random, edges were not as precise as in the north. I associated these characteristics with Italians rather than Swiss Germans.

9. This is not low density by some community standards, where two or three units per acre is the norm, but to be considered "urban," I believe an area must have at least fifteen dwelling units per net residential acre.

10. James S. Duncan, Jr., "Landscape and the Communication of Social Identity," in *The Mutual Interaction of People and Their Built Environment,* ed. Amos Rapoport (The Hague: Mouton, 1976).

11. Kevin Lynch, Donald Appleyard, *Signs in the City,* (Cambridge, Mass.: MIT Press, 1963).

12. Lynn H. Lofland, "The Modern City: Spatial Ordering," in *Environmental Psychology: People and Their Physical Settings,* 2nd ed., ed. Harold M. Proshansky (New York: Holt, Rinehart and Winston, 1976).

13. Allan B. Jacobs, "They're Locking the Doors to Downtown," *Urban Design International* 1 (July/August 1980).

14. Clay, *Close-Up*, p. 85 ff. Clay gives a wonderful characterization of strip commercial areas.

15. For the downtown area as a special destination for the traveler, see John Brinkerhoff Jackson, "The Stranger's Path," in *Landscapes: Selected Writings of J. B. Jackson,* ed. Ervin H. Zube (Amherst: University of Massachusetts Press, 1970).

16. Boris S. Pushkarev and Jeffrey M. Zupan, *Public Transportation and Land Use Policy* (Bloomington: Indiana University Press, 1977).

17. Donald Appleyard, *Livable Streets,* Protected Neighborhoods (Berkeley: University of California Press, 1981).

18. For a short, excellent discussion of the physical form and human satisfaction and values, see Kevin Lynch, *A Theory of Good City Form* (Cambridge, Mass.: MIT Press, 1981), chap. 5.

19. Hans Blumenfeld, "Correlation between Value of Dwelling Units and Altitude," *Land Economics* (November 1948).

20. See William Alonso, *Location and Land Use* (Cambridge, Mass.: Harvard University Press, 1964), or Colin Clark, *Population Growth and Land Use* (New York: St. Martin's Press, 1968), chap. 9, or, for a succinct overview, Lynch, *Theory of Good City Form.*

21. Peirce F. Lewis, "Axioms for Reading the Landscape," in *The Interpretation of Ordinary Landscapes,* ed. D.W. Meinig (New York: Oxford University Press, 1979).

22. Ibid.

23. If the windows all have different types of curtains and bric-a-brac, we guess that each window represents a separate unit, whose dimensions can then be estimated. Or a glance into a back door may reveal electric meters for each unit; the units must be small if so many are in the building.

24. This includes the values of the pressure groups that may set those standards, which then benefit that group. Good examples can be found in standards for plumbing, building materials, sizes of school rooms and school sites, and street widths.

4. Observing and Interpreting East Walnut Hills

1. Ralph Bolton, Martin Griesel, April Laskey, Don Lenz, and Charles Lohre.

6. Observing the Unknown

1. A detailed description of each case study is in preparation, to be published by the Institute of Urban and Regional Development, University of California, Berkeley.

2. The Nolli map shows vineyard and agricultural uses in the 1700s: Gianbattista Nolli, "Roma Al Tempo Di Benedetto XIV, La Pianta Di Roma—del 1748," Città del Vaticano.

3. In fact, the units are not small by American standards, which would have been apparent if I had measured them by pacing. Instead, I assumed that Italian dwellings would be smaller than American dwellings. Also, I observed that people were expanding the units onto balconies.

4. A fourth Italian case study was carried out in Milan at approximately the same time as the Bologna study. The observed area of Milan is larger, but in historical development, physical clues, and public policies guiding current

developments, it is quite similar to this area of Bologna. Because of the similarities, I concentrate here on Bologna, with digressions to Milan for illumination (a Bolognese might not appreciate that word in this context).

5. In Milan the problem was the same: a concentration of new trucking firms in one area was not seen because the major truck destination was just beyond the study area.

6. The timing sequence—private buildings first, followed by public development—is similar to that of the Diamond Heights redevelopment project in San Francisco in the 1960s, which successfully achieved economic and racial integration.

7. In Milan I was not aware that in 1923 the city had annexed Affori, an independent socialist settlement dating back to medieval times, in order to eliminate its political base. The political reasons for physical boundaries is important, particularly where they are part and parcel of major development strategies.

7. Looking Back

1. Kevin Lynch and Donald Appleyard, *Temporary Paradise? A Look at the Special Landscape of the San Diego Region* (Massachusetts Institute of Technology, 1974).

2. Many cities publish booklets to help residents with home repairs. See *Rehab Right: How to Rehabilitate Your Oakland House without Sacrificing Architectural Assets* (Oakland, Calif.: City of Oakland Planning Department, June 1978).

3. Allan B. Jacobs, *Making City Planning Work* (Chicago: American Society of Planning Officials, 1978), pp. 88–89.

Index